efore

SKILLS TRAINING FOR
COUNSELLING

'6

SKILLS TRAINING FOR COUNSELLING

Francesca Inskipp

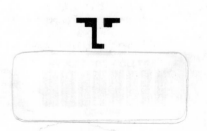

Cassell

Wellington House   127 West 24th Street
125 Strand   New York
London WC2R 0BB   NY 10011

© Francesca Inskipp 1996

British Library Cataloguing-in-Publication Data
A catalogue record for this book is available from the British Library

First published 1996, Reprinted 1996

ISBN 0–304–32920–7 (hardback)
0–304–32918–5 (paperback)

Typeset by Chapter One (London)
Printed and bound in Great Britain by
Redwood Books Limited, Trowbridge, Wiltshire

Contents

Foreword

I first trained as a counsellor in 1975. Since that time interest in counselling in Britain has mushroomed. For example, membership of the British Association for Counselling (BAC) continues to grow and training courses in counselling are cropping up everywhere. Fortunately, this growth in the development of counselling in Britain has been paralleled by an increasing concern that counsellors need to be properly trained and their work professionally supervised. The Counsellor Trainer and Supervisor series is designed to reflect this developing interest in the training and supervision of counsellors. It is the first series in Britain devoted to these two important and related professional activities and seeks to provide a forum for leading counsellor trainers and supervisors to share their experiences with their novice and more experienced colleagues.

Counsellor trainers place a great deal of emphasis on helping trainee counsellors to acquire and develop competence in a broad range of counselling skills. Francesca Inskipp has been at the forefront of counselling skills training for many years and in this book she shares her varied experience of this pivotal part of counsellor training.

Counsellors preparing to assume a training role will find much of value to help them integrate counselling skills training into the curriculum of a professional counsellor training course. In addition this book will provide many helpful hints and much encouragement to those concerned with training a broad range of helpers in counselling skills. This most practical book will also stimulate experienced counsellor trainers to reflect helpfully on their current training practice.

Windy Dryden

Introduction

My first reaction on being asked to write a book on counselling skills for trainers was 'not another – is there any more to say?'. On reflection there is more to say. This book is about skills and competencies for counsellors, aimed at trainers who run diploma or masters' courses which produce counsellors, as distinct from courses which train in counselling skills for people in the helping professions who are not wearing the label 'counsellor'.

My continued interest and involvement in this area has come from issues raised in four areas of my present work: as supervisor/consultant for several counsellor trainers who run counsellor diploma courses; as external assessor/moderator for diploma courses; as consultant for courses planning to apply for British Association for Counselling (BAC) recognition; as a member of BAC panels responsible for recognizing courses. My involvement in setting up the BAC recognition of trainers also raised the questions 'What is a good skills trainer?' and 'How do you train trainers?'.

Some of the issues raised in consultation and supervision with trainers would seem important to explore in this book. One very current issue is how the competencies set up by the Advice, Guidance and Counselling Lead Body concerned with National Vocational Qualifications will affect counsellor training. Will training courses adopt NVQs as part or all of their assessment scheme? How might present course assessments tie up with competencies? Training for competencies can also lead to a much wider concept of skills training, for example to include skills of self-awareness and self-management in skills training.

There are also questions on how new developments in the field of counselling are affecting skills training. Many courses are now teaching an integrative or eclectic model of counselling, embracing two or more theories, and this has implications for the skills taught. The need for many counsellors to be involved in brief or time-limited counselling raises the question of whether all counsellors should have some training in this and especially in the relevant skills.

Another development in the field is the move for students to be more responsible for designing and assessing their learning on the course – what and how they will learn. There is a continuum in courses from completely student managed and designed to completely staff managed, with many variations in between. It occurs to me that this book could be useful for students who are on student-managed courses and want to be involved in planning how and what they want to learn in order to become competent counsellors. It could save inventing some wheels again, and it could be a starting point for creating exciting new learning packages.

Perhaps one urgent area for consideration is the current public criticism levelled at counsellors. The rapid development of many new courses producing many new counsellors may be producing quantity rather than quality. If we are to try to ensure that the counsellors who leave our courses stamped with a qualification are really competent to help clients, we need to be constantly seeking to improve the quality of our training and seeking to validate that we do produce competent, compassionate counsellors who can work in a rapidly changing world. Carkhuff's reminder (Carkhuff, 1969a) that some counsellors can make clients worse rather than helping them, challenges us to develop higher training standards which deliver competent counsellors. Carkhuff (Carkhuff, 1969b) also found that some trainers who function on the core qualities at a low level, make their students worse rather than better counsellors; this means we need to look to our professional skills and how we are maintaining and developing our competence.

The book is a mixture of ideas and issues, stemming from talking and working with fellow trainers and students in the years since I first started a diploma course in 1973; I would like to thank them for the inspiration, ideas and creativity we have shared. I have been fortunate in being involved in many of the exciting developments which have taken place in these years, especially in the raising of standards in training courses as a result of the BAC Schemes for the Recognition of Courses, Supervisors and Trainers. I hope this book will stimulate new developments in skills training for counsellors – there is still a long way to go. Some of the ideas for training may seem prescriptive; they are not meant to be, but are presented as shared ideas to be possibly built into your own style or ignored. Each chapter ends with a list of questions which could be used for discussion by trainers and students – and maybe clients.

The book is arranged in eight chapters, beginning with some history of skills training, some frameworks for teaching and learning skills, the place of skills in the curriculum, then preparation for teaching and for setting up a learning group, some ideas on teaching the competencies and assessing, with a final chapter on trainer competencies. The appendices contain some further practical ideas for skills learning and for identifying competencies as a method of assessment.

The examples I have used in this book have been taken from my work with trainers and courses; they are an amalgam of issues raised, and ideas shared. To illustrate issues and ideas I have created four fictional courses with four fictional trainers. Trainers may try to recognize themselves, or their colleagues, but I reiterate that the courses and trainers exist only in my imagination. The four trainers and their courses are:

- Pauline; a two-year diploma course, Egan-based with a leaning towards person-centred.
- Shirley; a two-year diploma course, integrative – person-centred with Gestalt and Transactional Analysis (TA).
- Brian; a three-year diploma course, psycho-dynamic.
- Robert; a two-year diploma course, Egan-based with some cognitive-behavioural.

ONE

Which skills?
Which competencies?

This chapter gives a brief overview of the development of counsellor skills training, including the rise of National Vocational Qualifications and the development of competencies. There is a suggested list of Competencies in Table 1.1 on p.6.

Being competent at skills does not necessarily make a good counsellor, but a counsellor with poor skills is not likely to be helpful to his or her clients. Similarly, competence at skills does not make a good trainer, but a trainer with poor training skills may do more harm than good to students.

Perhaps we should ask first what is the place of skills training in the education of a counsellor and how has this training developed? When I first trained in counselling 25 years ago at the University of Keele, skills were just beginning to be introduced in this country. We learnt that 'mirroring' was the way to demonstrate empathy, unconditional positive regard and congruence. An American behaviourist introduced us to our first skills exercises or mirroring, paraphrasing and giving feedback to each other – a very frightening experience. Then Robert Carkhuff visited us and said the three 'conditions' were not enough and introduced us to further skills. This was at the end of our course and we did not have opportunities to practise these latter skills – and 25 years later I still find that is the case on some courses.

In these 25 years I have seen – and been part of – a revolution which has made basic skills a necessary and central part of counsellor training – and of the training of many helping professionals and volunteers. The ability to give attention, listen, reflect, paraphrase and summarize has become the bedrock on which counselling rests. 'If you can't do that you can't counsel' has been my clarion call. Starting to write this book makes me consider whether this is true – and further, if you can only do that, can you call yourself a counsellor? What research backs this up? Our skills training has been imported from the United States where there has been considerable research, and perhaps it is useful to see how skills training developed there.

Rogers (1957) was the first person to move the training of counsellors out of the realm of the mysterious into the realm of the observable and trainable by making audiotape recordings of sessions. He says in *A Way of Being* (Rogers, 1980, p. 138):

> Then came my transition to a full-time position at Ohio State University, where, with the help of students, I was at last able to scrounge equipment for recording my and my students' interviews. I cannot exaggerate the excitement of our learnings as we clustered about the machine that enabled us to listen to ourselves, playing over and over some puzzling point at which the interview clearly went wrong, or those moments in which the client moved significantly forward.

Roger's work on the core conditions – empathic understanding, unconditional positive regard and genuineness – stimulated researchers to assess the extent to which the counsellor used these conditions and in 1967 Truax and Carkhuff began research on developing programmes of didactic-experiential training to teach communication of the 'facilitative conditions'.

Carkhuff's Human Resource Training was originally developed to train Rogerian or client-centred counsellors and it has been very influential in the US in counsellor education programmes. In 1969 'concreteness', 'self-disclosure', 'confrontation' and 'immediacy', referred to as the 'initiative' or 'action' conditions, were added to the initial list of core conditions (Carkhuff, 1969a, 1969b) and in 1976 problem solving and programme development skills were also added (Carkhuff and Berenson, 1976).

Carkhuff originally identified two types of skills for helpers – 'discrimination', the ability to hear, understand and pick out the essential thoughts or feelings which were being expressed, and 'communication', the ability to communicate empathy, respect and warmth. He used a scale of 1–5 to identify levels of ability in these two skills and developed tests which could be used in the selection of helpers and as pre- and post-training evaluation (Carkuff, 1969a). He believed it was important to select helpers for training who already had these skills to some extent. He also said that trainers who were at a low level on these skills could make trainees worse rather than better.

This systematic training included didactic presentation and demonstration of each individual skill followed by experiential learning and practice. There was also great importance placed on the self-development of the trainees; they participated in a group facilitated by trainers who provided high facilitative conditions for members and modelled the core conditions of empathy, unconditional positive regard and congruence. The two components emphasized the importance of integrating theoretical and skills learning with personal growth.

Microcounselling was developed by Ivey in 1968 (Ivey, 1971). The micro-counselling programme introduced the idea of identifying clearly delineated discrete behaviours such as attending, reflection of feeling, summarizing or self-disclosure, and teaching them systematically, one at a time, and then integrating them. The training model takes beginning counsellors through a series of didactic and experiential skills exercises with supervised practice and immediate concrete feedback. From this it is hoped that they will eventually be able to engage competently in a broad base of theoretical approaches – from psycho-dynamic to rational emotive. Ivey demonstrated that with this training, para-professionals could be trained to provide the core facilitative conditions for clients without a long psychological counselling training, and so caused a minor revolution in professional training. It is his work which has shaped much of the counselling skills training in this country.

Kagan (1975) is the third influence with his *Interpersonal Process Recall* (IPR) system of training. This is not focused on teaching specific communication skills; the core of IPR is a unique recall process in which an 'inquirer' guides counselling trainees as they review their video- or audio-recorded sessions with clients. It is based on the theory that even beginning counsellors perceive and understand much more of their communication with the client than might be expected. Also, beginning counsellors often miss parts of interviews because of performance anxiety and preoccupation with what impression they are making – IPR can help to reduce anxiety.

The overall purpose is to encourage students to become more aware of the interaction process, to study their own interpersonal behaviour and become more attuned to their own sensations and thoughts in a safe recall situation. In developing this awareness by recall outside the session, they become more aware in the actual session, and can learn to use this to develop the counselling relationship. They may also become aware of what promotes their anxieties and so more able to deal with the anxiety and work more authentically with the client. This training method has not had such an impact on training in Britain, partly because it is more time consuming and not easy to incorporate into basic counselling skills courses. However, it has great potential for developing the skills which depend on internal and interpersonal awareness, e.g. 'self-disclosure and 'immediacy', it can help trainees identify the kind of interactions which may be difficult for them, and give them opportunities to rehearse appropriate interventions with future clients.

Some research has been carried out in the US on the effectiveness of these three methods of training (Baker *et al.*, 1990). Some of this research seems to show that students learn skills by these methods, especially by microcounselling, but may also lose them over time and revert to their original ways of responding. Connor (1994) gives detailed references to the main research on skills training, in both the UK and the US, most of which shows that micro-skill methods of learning can produce skilled communicators.

In 1975 Gerard Egan (Egan, 1975) brought together all the above work and produced explicit lists of skills for what he defined as a Three-stage Model for Helping, with specific skills for each stage:

1. Helping a client explore himself and his situation.
2. Helping him come to a deeper understanding.
3. Helping him move to action.

This systematic model has had a great influence in the UK on the development of skills training, both within courses for counsellors and in courses of counselling skills for helpers generally. The model has been revised by Egan in four subsequent editions of the *Skilled Helper* with some revision of the stages and of the skills.

The development of skills training in counsellor courses was paralleled by an upsurge of counselling skills training for people in the helping professions and voluntary organizations who saw counselling as part of their work. With this upsurge has also come the development, mainly by the British Association for Counselling (BAC), of the gradual professionalization of counselling by developing schemes for the accreditation of counsellors and the recognition of supervisors and training courses for counsellors.

This in turn has led to a need to differentiate between counselling skills and counselling – who is trained or qualified to do what – and this leads us to the impact of National Vocational Qualifications (NVQs) on the counselling field.

NVQs were introduced following the 1986 White Paper 'Working Together – Education and Training' in order to establish a nationally recognized and defined structure for standards and competencies of vocational qualifications. The intention was to bridge the gap between vocational qualifications and academic qualifications. Many existing elements of good practice by workers were unrecognized through any form of qualification, while academic recognition did not necessarily equate to relevant or specific competence.

In 1993 a 'Lead Body' was set up to cover advice, guidance and counselling to produce occupational standards and performance criteria which would be used to give recognition and accreditation to practitioners across this field. This could affect the present systems of accreditation and professional registration which is under much discussion at the present time.

As a preliminary to developing the standards a differentiation project (Russell *et al.*, 1992) was set up which separated the different roles of befriending, advice, guidance, the use of counselling skills, and counselling to see which competencies would be similar in each case, and which would be different. One important difference identified is that 'counselling skills may be used in any helping role and are seen as "high level communication, interpersonal and social skills used intentionally in a manner consistent with the goals and values of counselling ethics"'. Counselling overlaps with this, but 'there is a specific *role* of counsellor which "is clearly and explicitly contracted, and the boundaries of the relationship identified"'. From this document, competencies which are specific to the counsellor role have been identified, as well as those which overlap with the other roles. A further development has been the identification of competencies for psychotherapists which overlap – or are identical – with counselling competencies, and also competencies for couple counselling, for group work, and for telephone counselling. These competencies have been defined in terms of outcomes to the client, the key purpose of the work of the counsellor.

However, there is considerable debate among counsellors and counsellor trainers as to whether it is possible to define or assess a counsellor by competencies. Is counselling an art rather than a science? (Russell and Dexter, 1993); all these will be important issues in the development of counsellor training. Skills training can produce a technician with a bag of tools for his or her trade; how and when to use those skills with a client needs education – the development of the attitudes and qualities of a counsellor, the internalizing of theoretical concepts, the understanding of self and an ability to communicate to self and others what is being done and for what purpose. Skills training then, needs to be closely tied to the rest of the course but also needs to be seen as a specific course of skills which can be broken down into discrete micro-skills, learnt and practised. It is not possible to use skills fluently and with competence by learning about them, but only by having a good model to know what they look like and sound like, then practising them with feedback, probably putting them together into mega-skills and then understanding how and when to use them according to the theory being used. The BAC has affirmed the importance of skills training in their Course Recognition and Counsellor Accreditation regulations by stating that there must be 200 hours of skills training for accreditation as a counsellor.

So, what is a competent, skilled counsellor who can reliably be expected to help not harm clients? What sort of training can enable students to learn skills? What are the competencies a trainer needs to enable students to become competent counsellors? 'Competent' has been defined as 'properly qualified or skilled – adequately capable'; 'skill' as 'practical knowledge in combination with ability' or 'expertness, practised ability, facility in an action'. Competencies could be looked at as tasks which need to be broken down into skills for learning and practising. Each competency can also be looked at as open-ended in terms of its achievement and its manner of achievement; there need to be criteria for reaching a certain level which is 'good enough' and can be assessed. However, to become a competent counsellor seems to me to be a life-long goal and competency could thus be seen as competency to learn – not a static state.

Are there 'core' skills which every counsellor should develop, irrespective of the particular theoretical orientation of the course? From exploring a range of courses it would seem there are core skills, though there will be differences in emphasis, and each course will need to define the particular skills needed for their particular theory.

Of the myriad theories of counselling and psychotherapy, no research has proved that one theory is more effective at helping all clients, though it seems generally agreed that being able to set up a working relationship by communicating the core qualities of empathy, acceptance and genuineness are essential underpinnings for any counselling – and for any training. Recent writing seems to indicate that matching clients to different theories may be better than trying to use one model with all clients and all issues. This implies counsellor familiarity and skills with several models, and the ability to match them to the client.

Some trainers are now beginning to set out training objectives in terms of competencies. From consultancy with a variety of trainers and courses, I have taken a wider look at skills and competencies which seem necessary for a qualified counsellor, and a list of these is set out in Table 1.1. I have combined with these the Competencies for Counsellors and Psychotherapists defined in recent work on NVQs. These Competencies are still being tested in the field so by the time this book is published there may be some alteration, and there is a lot more work to be done on setting up performance criteria for assessing competence.

Table 1.1 *List of Tasks, Skills and Competencies*

---

1. Meet and contract with the client – begin to build a working alliance
        Client assessment skills
        Introduce self and counselling
        Negotiate a working agreement
        Begin to build a working relationship
  NVQs: B. 8. Ensure a structured counselling relationship
            1. Establish boundaries of professional relationship
            2. Facilitate a mutual overview of the relationship
            3. Establish the counselling contract
      B.16. Explore the potential for a therapeutic relationship

2. Develop, maintain and end a counselling relationship
        Communicate empathy, acceptance/respect, genuineness/openness
        Review, amend, repair if necessary or possible
        Recognize/make explicit/work with transference and counter-transference
        End the relationship

NVQs: B. 9. Establish and maintain a counselling relationship
  B.18. Use a therapeutic relationship to work through client's concerns
      1. Develop the therapeutic relationship
      2. Manage power aspects of the therapeutic relationship
      3. Respond to client's feelings in the therapeutic relationship
      4. Work through client's concerns
      5. Move therapeutic relationship forward
  B.19. Sustain and monitor the therapeutic relationship
      3. Develop understanding of the therapeutic relationship
      4. Achieve best possible ending of the therapeutic relationship

3. Work in a session

Use counselling skills
    (a) to assist client to work on concerns
    (b) to empower client
    (c) to develop and maintain interaction with client
Help client work on concerns by
    (a) Using the counselling relationship and the interaction as it happens
    (b) Selecting and using specific skills from specific theoretical orientation
Monitor progress of the client, review and recontract if necessary
Operate within professional codes
Pace the session and bring to a close

NVQs: B.11. 1. Enable client to identify concerns
      2. Enable client to work through concerns
      3. Monitor the counselling process
      4. Bring counselling process to an end
  B.12. 3. Identify own theoretical orientation and its implications on the counselling process
  B.20. Utilize a theoretical model
      1. Choose an appropriate theoretical model
      2. Use theoretical model to understand clients
      3. Use theoretical model to understand and inform own practice
      4. Evaluate practice against theoretical model

4. Develop self-awareness skills within the counselling session

Develop self-scanning skills
Sort sensations and communicate appropriately to client
Develop awareness of 'process'
Communicate awareness appropriately

NVQ : B.12. Monitor self within the counselling process
      1. Differentiate between own internal world and that of the client
      2. Monitor own effect on the client

5. Manage self
        Clarify own values, beliefs, attitudes and ethical codes
        Manage own physical, emotional, mental and spiritual life
        Commit self to continued professional development
NVQ: A. 4. 2. Ensure continual professional development
        A. 4. 6. Manage own use of time

6. Reflecting, monitoring, recording, using supervision
        Devise and use methods for reflecting on and recording work with client
        Prepare for and use supervision
NVQs: A. 4. Monitor and evaluate own work
        B.12. 4. Ensure continuing self-support and supervision

7. Develop referral procedures
        Know own limits of competence
        Develop referral register
        Negotiate referral with client
        Receive referrals appropriately
NVQs: A. 8. Operate referral procedures
        1. Identify sources of referrals
        2. Refer clients to other sources
        3. Receive referrals from other sources

8. Work in an organization/agency
        Negotiate a contract clarifying professional responsibilities and boundaries
        Give information appropriately and manage confidentiality
        Use group skills to communicate as a team member
NVQs: A. 9. Collect, process and manage information
        2. Interpret and provide information for use by others
        Provide feedback to other parties
        Participate in inter-agency information networks

9. Work as a freelance counsellor
        Set up suitable accommodation
        Publicize self and the service
        Use business skills, keep accounts, tax returns
        Set up support and accountability

Some of the competencies in the list have not traditionally been included in skills training sessions and it may be worthwhile for the reader to consider where they should be placed in a course, or whether some of them should be viewed as skills. Some might be included in supervision, personal development work, experiential theory work or professional studies, rather than in sessions labelled skills training, and if they are shared among the staff it would seem important to have clear agreement as to who is responsible for teaching and assessing them. Amongst different counsellor trainers there was a wide variation as to where the different skills were taught in the curriculum – and in some cases they were not taught as skills at all.

Nos. 2 and 3 'Developing a relationship' and 'Working in the session' were what was usually taught in skills sessions. In the main, no. 4 'Self-awareness' and no 5. 'Self-management skills' were often not taught specifically, but were hopefully developed as part of personal development groups, within personal counselling or by personal or learning journals. No.1 'Meeting and contracting with the client' was sometimes taught in supervision, sometimes in a section called 'Professional Practice', and sometimes in the skills training. Nos 6, 7, 8 and 9 when they were taught were in supervision or in 'Professional Practice'.

In some cases there was very little teaching of the specific skills and techniques relating to the core theory of the course. What was done was often included in experiential work done in theory sessions. Students learn about techniques related to theory, but do not always see them demonstrated and broken down into discrete skills, and with time given to understanding when and how to use them.

In later chapters I look in detail at each block of competencies and the skills which are contained within them, together with the skills and competencies needed by the trainer, and in Chapter 2 I consider some of the issues and frameworks for helping adults learn.

CHAPTER QUESTIONS

1. How do you define/assess a 'competent counsellor'?
2. Can important aspects of counsellor competency be rationally defined or rationally assessed, e.g. empathy, warmth, being present?
3. Which aspects of counsellor training could be defined as skills; which could not?
4. Can competencies defined for NVQs be used to assess and qualify a counsellor?
5. Should trainers embrace or ignore NVQs?
6. What are your beliefs about 'core skills', skills for 'integrative theories'?
7. Which of the competencies in the competency list (Table 1.1) would you include as skills work in your course?

TWO
Frameworks and issues for adult and skills learning

Skills training ... is likely to be one of the most threatening of their activities and has therefore to be approached with delicacy and with a regard for individual differences ... Trainers have to exhibit both firmness and gentleness if all participants are eventually to benefit from the various learning situations. (Dryden and Thorne, 1991, p. 7)

This chapter explores some of the issues around adult learning and looks at a skills learning cycle as a useful framework to understand and work with some of the difficulties.

Skills training is a challenge to you as a trainer, needing knowledge, technical skill and creative artistry to help students develop into skilled counsellors. Learning to set up counselling skills training has probably been the most significant learning for me during my career in counselling. I had gone to Keele University in 1970 with a brief to return to Essex to teach counselling to youth and community workers. Counselling which had been something every youth worker 'did' had now become something you had to go to university to learn, so I was despatched to discover the mysteries.

Reading Ivey's work on microcounselling, especially the research on teaching the skills to medical para-professionals, gave me hope and ideas; Carkhuff's visit demonstrating his models of training further clarified how to break down the skills into a structured learning programme and Gilmore (1973) gave me a structure for practice and feedback. All this has been very useful to me, and to my colleagues; however, structured learning and clear programmes can create difficulties – both because it can be 'imposed' learning and because it may not take enough account of individual differences.

So, before looking in detail at skill learning, I am setting out here some frameworks and thoughts on adult learning. A knowledge of some theories of adult and skill learning can help you plan structures which will allow for anxieties and fears to be diminished to a manageable level; new learning can be established and consolidated before moving on. Adult and skills learning has been studied and written about extensively and as a trainer you are probably familiar with some of the theories. However, I think it is useful to revise some of them briefly here and give references for more detailed follow-up.

Learning can be defined as 'a change in a person's behaviour resulting from experience' – so proof of learning is demonstrated by some change in the way a person is or what he or she does. What the person does can be observed and assessed, what he or she is, e.g. in terms of beliefs or attitudes, may be more difficult to observe or assess. Developing skills as a counsellor requires changes in both 'being' and 'doing' and this has implications for teaching and assessing.

• Some issues around adult learning

1. Adults bring established learning strategies and expectations formed from previous experience of learning at school or after. Some may want to be 'passive learners' and may have to be weaned to become active learners, to take responsibility for their own learning. Some may resent being 'told' and want to learn everything by discovery, although they may not know what there is to be discovered.

2. Giving some responsibility for what and how they will learn helps to keep students in adult role, rather than reverting to child which may bring up fears and resistances. Or, being 'made' to be responsible for their own learning may bring up other resistances.

3. Adults need to see the whole picture and the purpose – where the particular skill fits in, where this relates to other learning on the course and how their work with clients will benefit.

4. They need to be able to fit new learning into their present beliefs and frameworks for seeing the world. For example, if they are learning to reflect and paraphrase rather than ask questions they may have to be able to change their belief that asking questions is the best way to help clients to talk about themselves.

5. Many people learn best from experiencing and doing. Skills are learnt by practice and experiencing the results of that practice. Kolb (1976) gives a model of experiential learning in four steps:
   (a) concrete experience – what is happening;
   (b) reflective observation – what happened;

(c) abstract conceptualization – what does it mean;

(d) active experimentation – what shall I do as a result.

Using this model can be useful in designing experiential learning, to get the steps in the right order and to make sure they are all included. Dainow and Bailey (1988) give more details of designing skills learning using this model and Henderson in *Promoting Active Learning* (1989) gives further useful ideas.

● **Awareness of individual differences**

I have mentioned before that there is some research in this country on the effects – long-term and short-term – of the structured systematic training in counselling skills which we set up in faith. More needs to be done specifically in relation to the training of counsellors, and, in relation to individual differences, we perhaps should be asking 'For whom and under what conditions is systematic counselling training most useful or most effective?' Below are some thoughts on individual differences which may affect learning and which could help you consider possible issues arising in your skills groups.

1. *Learning styles*
   Honey (1986) cites four learning styles:
   — (a) activists – those who thrive on new experiences and active learning;
   — (b) reflectors – those who prefer time for thorough explorations and review;
   — (c) theorists – those who enjoy logical and integrated explorations within rational schema;
   — (d) pragmatists – those who like to apply ideas to see if they work.
   You will probably have a range of these styles among the individuals on your course and it can be useful to consider which individual will react positively or negatively to the structures you set up for skills learning.

2. *Developmental stages*
   We know, or think we know, that structured systematic training in skills works well on the whole, with beginning counsellor students. Research on supervision (Stoltenberg and Delworth, 1987) shows that counsellors in different developmental stages have different learning needs. Do students in different developmental stages require different kinds of training as they develop and become more autonomous?

3. *Gender*

   Another consideration is gender issues. Some research (Belenky et al., 1986) suggests that the two genders have different ways of 'knowing', or receiving, transmitting, and processing information. Some authors speculate that it is the masculine element that allows an individual to be logical and fluent in communication; the feminine element may often result in a loss for words in attempting to describe an experience. Is a systematic training approach that requires the production of a particular verbal response more consistent with the masculine rather than the feminine element within an individual? If so, where does the feminine energy get supported, validated and expressed in this particular mode of training?

4. *Culture, class*

   Lastly, the training methods were devised in the US for a white middle-class population of students and in this country the great proportion of students coming into counsellor courses are white and middle class. These training methods may work well on the whole with that population, but if we are to extend opportunities to a population from a much wider range of cultures and classes perhaps we need to research whether the structured systematic training is applicable to all – and if not what other methods of training in skills might be developed.

These are reflections which I hope you may pursue and perhaps consider, especially if you find some blocks in setting up training with some students.

A SKILLS LEARNING CYCLE

Having thought about some of the difficulties it is useful to think about what encourages, stimulates and supports new learning. When there are difficulties, how can we as trainers help students find creative ways to struggle with the difficulties and learn from them? A framework I have found helpful is a four-stage one of 'conscious competency' (Robinson, 1974).

Learners start from *unconscious incompetence;* they do not know what they do not know. Then they are presented with a new idea, new skill, new situation which requires them to think or act differently – they become *consciously incompetent.* This can be a very uncomfortable stage of feeling deskilled and inadequate as a person. The learners begin to recognize whether they want to become competent. To remove the discomfort, they will have to try new strategies, new ways of thinking, being, acting.

This can be particularly uncomfortable if students arrive already counselling and want to be confirmed that what they are doing is all right. It needs sensitive feedback affirming them as people and helping them recognize that they have some skills as well as deficits of skill. If the motivation and support is strong enough, they struggle and learn and become *consciously competent*. For some, this is another uncomfortable stage as it feels unnatural, artificial, incongruent, they have to unlearn some of the old ways. For others, this is an exciting stage of mastering a new skill or knowledge.

If they continue to practise, gradually the new ways of being and doing become part of them, they arrive at being *unconsciously competent* and have grown a new skill, extended their life yet again. This cycle will continue with each new skill presented, as long as the person is flexible and creative enough to respond to their ever changing environment.

How does this relate to a skills group? One trainer remarked that although students had all done a basic counselling skills course, some had moved from being unconsciously competent back to unconsciously incompetent – the new skills learnt had slipped and they were back in old ways of communicating, forgetting the important 'active listening' skills. When asked to practise basic skills again it was painful for experienced students to become consciously incompetent. The consciously competent stage also brought complaints of feeling artificial, not genuine, and feeling they were pretending rather than being empathic and accepting. The learning cycle helped them see this as a stage which would eventually pass.

The stage of moving from consciously incompetent to consciously competent can be very hard, especially for some people, e.g. perfectionists. It is the stage, for some, of 'doing it wrong', failing, feeling clumsy, feeling humiliated or in some cases shamed, or it can be the stage of playing with new ideas or actions, risking trying out, celebrating the excitement of learning. There is a need to risk making mistakes, to learn how to learn, and this needs a climate of support, nurturing and challenge.

How individuals approach this seems to be connected often with their early developmental stages of learning; if there are blocks, it can be useful for students to explore this in more depth, either in their personal development groups or in their own counselling.

Clarkson (1994), in *The Achilles Syndrome, overcoming the secret fear of failure*, has presented some useful ideas for helping people learn and work through the competence stages. One suggestion she makes is that it is impossible to teach skills to students who feel 'silly' – she says make them feel 'smart' first. So, a trainer skill: find creative ways of helping students feel smart!

This highlights the importance of fostering self-esteem in students. Being made to 'perform' and then not doing it well can seem disastrous for some students. Giving very clear models and instructions and starting with simple skills can build confidence in the early stages – and giving opportunities to practise without observers at first can also help to prevent esteem dropping.

Clarkson also suggests that it is difficult or impossible to train skills from an unconsciously competent stance – we need to return to the consciously competent stage so that we can break down and explain the skill in detail. You may have noticed how hard it is for an experienced driver to teach a learner how to drive a car – a frustrating experience for both of them.

I think helping students explore the learning cycle gives them a framework to understand some of the discomforts. I know in writing this book that the frustration of feeling stupid, inadequate, vulnerable, is helped by recognizing this as my conscious incompetent stage; it will pass if I do not give up. It does. And it will come again; I need to remember 'that passed, so will this'.

Learning requires curiosity and an appetite to learn – watch a small child struggling to walk or to climb or feed himself. How can we restimulate that childhood desire to struggle for competence? And without using competition as the motivation – instead the motivation is to achieve new skills and to be 'the best self I can be' to serve the clients.

Playing and creating fun in skills work can encourage learning and can be an effective way to reduce anxiety and promote risk-taking. Role-play, if introduced carefully, can provide playful learning opportunities, e.g. in introducing video work to terrified students, asking them to play the worst counsellor they could, or ham up the skills 'over the top'. Learning can be stimulated by clarifying the competencies they need to reach for the diploma and identifying the support they can obtain from the staff and from each other. Sometimes the list of competencies can be overwhelming, but for most students a clear picture of where they are heading and ideas of how they will get there is supportive, and challenging.

Because the skills need to be learnt and practised in specific sessions, the most important skill is then to be able to integrate the learnt skills into appropriate use with a client. This means confidence in performance and then choosing which skill to use when. This skill of integration and choosing, and choosing sometimes when stressed, is difficult to teach, but essential if we are to produce aware counsellors, not competent technicians. This is the art of training.

Probably the most important support for learning is to be in a safe group where the core qualities of empathy, respect and congruence are communicated by the trainer and by the students to each other, and where each student feels known and accepted. This demands skills from the trainers which we will look at in detail later. In the meantime the next consideration is where does all this fit into the curriculum.

CHAPTER QUESTIONS

1. How might you become aware of the different learning styles (Honey) in your group of students? What is your own preferred learning style?
2. How did you learn counselling skills and what worked well and not so well for you?
3. Can you identify developmental stages in your trainees? How might this affect your design of training?
4. Are you aware of whether your masculine or feminine element predominates in you as a trainer?
5. What might you do to become more aware of whether your training suits all cultures and classes?

THREE
The place of skills training in the curriculum

This chapter looks at where skills training fits into the overall course, who will teach and what structures need to be set up, and how this might be negotiated with staff and students.

Before the skills training is set up there are important preliminaries to explore, discuss and agree with the course team, and to publicize relevant items to students.

- What skills will be taught where in the curriculum?
- How will the content of the skills training relate to the rest of the course?
- In what structures will the skills be taught?
- If the students are to work in small groups, how will that be organized? Will the students choose their own groups or be allocated to a group?
- Who will teach skills? Will it be co-tutoring, team teaching?
- How will they be taught? Is there a team policy?
- How much responsibility for 'what' and 'how' will be allocated to students, and how much to tutors?
- How will individual students get feedback on their skill performance? Will it be shared among self, peers, tutors?
- Who will be responsible for final assessments? Is there a half-way assessment which can block students proceeding with the course?
- How will the final assessment be done?
- Will the external assessor be involved in skills assessment? How?

All this, of course, is part of course design but it often needs a new look with each new group of students, and when new staff join the course, especially if they are to teach skills. There are important choices to be made and sometimes differences to be negotiated among staff. The course leader has an important function in helping the decision making. In some courses some of these decisions will be made with the students when there are likely to be more difficult negotiations.

WHAT SKILLS WILL BE TAUGHT WHERE IN THE CURRICULUM

I have already raised this in Chapter 1 in relation to the overall list of skills and competencies (Table 1.1). If you decide to work from this list now is the time to decide – or negotiate with students – which skills will be taught in sessions labelled 'skills training', and which skills will be allocated to other sections of the course. A flow-chart showing how the skills fit in with the rest of the course structure is useful, e.g. certain skills need to be taught before the students start seeing clients. Staff also need to negotiate who will be responsible for the different learning.

WHAT STRUCTURES AND WHICH STAFF

The BAC Code of Ethics and Practice for Trainers states:

> Training is at its most effective when there are two or more trainers to facilitate observation and evaluation. Trainers have a responsibility to ensure this as far as possible.
>
> The size of the group needs to be congruent with the training objectives and the model of working. For people seeking training in counselling or counselling skills it is considered that a maximum staff to student ratio of 1:12 is preferable.

In a large course students will need to be in groups of not more than 12 for skill practice so that each student can receive feedback from the tutor, besides any given by peers. It is often useful to teach skills in larger groups with two tutors who can share in modelling the skills and, if video models are used, these can be shown and talked about in the large group before breaking down into small groups for practice.

Below are some examples of structures trainers use for working with up to 24 students – and for working with 12 or fewer students.

Pauline, who works in a university department, said:

> I work with 24 students with a co-tutor and two trainee tutors. We work in a large group for several sessions, all four of us taking part, helping the group get to know each other, working in twos, threes and fours on clarifying what is to be learnt and how we will work together.

We then divide up into four groups of six and work in those small groups most of the time, coming together for general work. Those small groups are the practice and feedback group. The tutors meet briefly each week for exchange and twice a term for longer discussion of our learning and the students' progress. We are lucky to be able to pay trainee tutors a fee; most of them are counsellors who trained previously with us and already had good group and training experience.

Shirley, who works in a tertiary college, said:

I work with 22 students and a co-tutor. We split into two groups of 12 and 10 (to get even numbers). We let the students choose which group they go into, only stipulating there must be 10 and 12. This choosing usually takes up two whole skills sessions, but we think the learning which comes from the choosing is worth the time. We stay in these groups for the first year and then mix the groups up and alternate skills work with supervision. They choose four supervision groups and two of those come together for skills which makes the new mix.

Brian works in a counselling agency where they run their own diploma; he says:

We only recruit up to 12 students for each year and we work in one group for all sessions except supervision. We expect students to have learnt basic skills before they come on the course. Skills are closely related to theory and are practised in theory or supervision sessions. The students work in pairs or triads with an observer with a tutor listening in on the work. We use role-play in supervision to try out skills.

Robert works in an adult education department of a college; he says:

I work with 11 students this year – a difficult prime number but one student dropped out at the last moment. I start working with the whole group doing much as Pauline says she does for a few sessions. I then divide them into two groups of six and five and teach them the 'Gilmore' structure of working [see Appendix I]. I then spend half the session with each group and we work in these groups for four terms so the groups get very close. I bring them together every few sessions to work on new skills – using demonstration models and role-play. Self- and peer-assessment and learning plans are done within the groups; I make sure I see everybody practise within three or four sessions and give feedback. I see their learning plans and written assessments termly.
    Having heard Pauline on trainee tutors, I would very much like to institute this on my course, but money is short and I wonder if I could

find a tutor willing to work free for the experience – and one who has experienced Gilmore structure and could work in that way. With a trainee tutor I would still need to see both groups I think, at any rate until the tutor was more experienced in assessing.

NEGOTIATING STRUCTURES AND CONTENT WITH STUDENTS

I mentioned in the Introduction the range of courses from those in which students negotiate all their learning to those in which the timetable and content is completely staff-organized. In Chapter 2 I suggest that adults may learn best when they have some responsibility for deciding what and how they will learn. Below are some of the questions raised by tutors and examples given by different courses:

The course I teach on is student-managed; how do I negotiate to set up skill learning and practice sessions?

The answer is – often with difficulty! I asked Pauline who works in this way and she said:

> I came from a course which is self-managed and feel it has enormous strengths in the ethos of students taking responsibility for their own learning, sharing power, and I feel it encourages individuality. However, I have found that students have great resistance to setting up groups to learn and practise skills, especially those students who come with more experience. I think they are consciously or unconsciously very vulnerable to exposing their work to their peers; they often feel they know all the skills from basic courses and want to spend time on more advanced learning. I find I have now got tough and insisted in negotiating skills time. I also give them an expanded list of skills which goes beyond the basic so that they know what they will be expected to do to obtain their diploma. The list includes basics as I usually find many students have forgotten those, or got too unconsciously competent and cannot analyze and reflect on how they are working.

She added:

> As I look back on my own course I realize I missed out on a lot of skills training because we students did not want it and I have had to learn skills as I have taught them – and I realize how much it has improved my own counselling. So I feel justified in being tough about this and I see a big improvement in their skills as counsellors as we move through the training sessions.

One way to ensure skills training is included in student-managed courses may be to clarify the original contract in the student brochure or handbook. This should specify what competencies in skills must be reached at each stage of the course, clear goals for completion of the course with clear assessment procedures, and the resources you provide, including staff. Negotiation is then within these parameters.

Our course is structured with a clear timetable and syllabus for what is learnt when; how do I help students take more responsibility for their own learning?

Shirley, who works on a college course of this type, said:

> When I first joined the course I worked with a co-tutor who had established very clear structures and taught the three stages of skills set out by Egan in his early model. This worked, but somehow the feedback by students to each other felt too supportive and not challenging enough for them to really hone their skills. Feedback from the tutors was perceived as critical, and as a result I think we were not challenging enough. That tutor left and I have a new co-tutor who has very good group skills and wants to use the 'process' in the group to enable students to feel more responsible for each other's learning, and for their own. We have kept clear structures for learning first-stage skills but spend more time on exploring the process of feedback – what are the feelings? How do we know when a skill is well used? How can we be more genuine and authentic? How do we feel when we are not genuine and how does that relate to being with a client? This 'process' work leads us into working on the second-stage skills of disclosing feelings and thoughts appropriately, exploring the interaction as it is happening in 'immediacy' skills, and how 'deeper empathy' may be threatening when we do not want to be 'seen beneath'.
>
> We have given the students a list of skills to be assessed, how they will get feedback from us after each term and the expectation that they will keep a record of their progress and produce a statement of what they need to learn and practise next. We have also spent time clarifying with them how they will be assessed at the end, what criteria are used, and what weight peer assessment will have. We also let them know that their final assessment is on their use of the skills with clients – so they need to accustom themselves and their clients to audio-taping. All this seems to share more responsibility with them, and produces a lot of challenging learning for us!

All these courses are within the staff to student ratio limit of 1:12 set up by the BAC. Students have a right to complain to the BAC if courses exceed this limit in their skills training groups, provided the course is an organizational member of the BAC, or the tutors are individual members of the BAC.

The BAC in the 'Courses Recognition Guide' does not specify the number of hours required for skills training – it says 'substantial'. For BAC accreditation counsellors are required to have undergone at least 200 hours of skills training. To cover the competencies and skills set out above would probably need a minimum of 300 hours, but some of the competencies might well be learned under other course headings. It can be a good exercise for course teams to clarify how the hours are allocated.

INDIVIDUAL OR CO-TRAINERS

There are a lot of advantages in training as a pair and my richest learning experiences in training have come from working with a colleague. Training is often stressful and being able to share that, and to know that your co-trainer will pick up things you miss, can reflect on the session with you, and can be objective when you are submerged – all this makes co-training a good experience. The planning together and finding ways to work which support and challenge each other can benefit both the course and the professional development of the trainers. Students gain from having two personalities, two opinions, conflicting at times, and from having to relate to two 'authority' figures. The trainers need a good open relationship and good supervision to prevent being split into 'good' and 'bad', and basically to agree on methods of training and levels of assessment.

Individual trainers have the advantage of not having to agree methods and maybe compromise on what and how they want to teach. Planning joint training can also be more time consuming, especially with a new co-trainer. The dynamics of the group can be easier to manage as a single trainer and in co-training there can be stress in finding a balance of how you respond to the trainees and to each other.

Co-training, I think, is the finest way of learning for a new trainer – provided you have a good model to learn from and time for reflection together.

These are some of the preliminaries to sort out. The next things to look at are the preparations you will need to make to set up skills work and feedback structures. We look in detail at some of those in Chapter 4.

CHAPTER QUESTIONS

1. Where and how does skills training fit into your whole curriculum?
2. Are some tutors designated to teach skills? If so how are they chosen?
3. What is your attitude towards students planning and managing their own learning? What is the practice on your course?
4. What is your attitude towards staff-, peer- and self-assessment? What do you practise?
5. What do you do if you are required to take more than 12 students for skills training?
6. What is your attitude to co-training? What benefits or disadvantages might it have for you?

FOUR

Preparation for skills teaching

Below are some ideas which need consideration in preparing the skills work of the course:

- List the skills and break down to micro-skills.
- Work out the timetable for the time available.
- Assemble your resources.
- Prepare students to be clients for each other.
- Teach feedback skills.

BREAK DOWN EACH TASK INTO SKILLS

In Chapter 3 I suggest that you decide which skills would be taught where – quite a herculean task if you took all the list at the end of Chapter 1 (Table 1.1), but could be a useful staff – and student – exercise.

In the list in Table 1.1 there are tasks, skills and competencies. Some skills have already been broken down into micro-skills, e.g. the core skills which seem to be applicable to any counselling theory – the skills of attending, observing, listening, the 'active listening' skills of paraphrasing, reflecting, summarizing, which build into the mega-skills of communicating empathy and acceptance and building a relationship. It is necessary to break down other mega-skills, e.g. negotiating, into micro skills – listening, active listening, purpose stating, preference stating, questioning, summarizing etc. – so that they can be demonstrated and practised. It is then necessary to put the skills together so that they can be practised as a mega-skill and used appropriately. Dryden and Feltham (1994) states that 'Encouraging students to examine skills in great detail is a way of establishing an ability to supervise one's own work and to generate critical and creative thinking in relation to it'. Being able to name skills and having a shared vocabulary for them, makes feedback and learning possible.

The core skills above and ideas for teaching them, have been written about in detail over the last ten years and diploma students are usually expected to be familiar with these and able to demonstrate them. However, my experience of many courses is that these need revising and often reteaching. As I said above, I believe these skills are an essential base for the whole process of counselling, and competence in them is paramount. A list of these skills (mainly taken from Egan) is given in Table 4.1, and for more information on teaching these and for specific exercises and activities, see Inskipp (1993), Dainow and Bailey (1988) and Egan (1994).

Listing the skills that are to be learnt

I suggest in Chapter 3 that a checklist of all the tasks or competencies, perhaps taken from the list in Table 1.1, might be prepared, stating in which section of the curriculum they will be taught. These tasks or competencies will need to be broken down into specific skills (some, of course, will overlap with each other).

Table 4.1 gives an overall list of general counselling skills. You will need to add to these a list of the specific skills that are relevant to the model of counselling being taught. This will probably need to be a team task, or if it is delegated to the skills trainer, the team will need to endorse it. You may need to do quite a lot of trawling to gather all the skills that your particular model will need. If it is an integrative model you will need to be selective which skills are culled from the range of integrated theories.

WORK OUT THE TIMETABLE

Work out how much time you will spend on each section approximately and plan a rough timetable for the whole programme – some courses spend so long on early skills the rest are not practised enough or at all. This assumes you have already decided with the team which skills may be included in other sections of the course, e.g. self-management skills, self-awareness skills.

Timetabling the skills training session

It is not a good idea to put the skills session at the end of the teaching time. I have seen skills groups struggling at 8 p.m. after many of them have been working at work or home all the morning and learning from 1.30 p.m. – it is too difficult both for students and for tutors. Skills work

Table 4.1 *Communication and interpersonal skills*

First-stage skills

Helping the client explore his or her concerns and building a relationship by communicating empathic understanding, acceptance and genuineness by
 Attending
 Observing
 Listening
 Active listening
  Paraphrasing
  Reflecting feelings
  Summarizing

Negotiating
 Giving information
 Purpose stating
 Preference stating
Focusing/moving forward
 Questioning
 Asking to be specific/concrete
 Asking for contrasts
 Offering choice points

Second-stage skills

Deepening understanding by
 Communicating deeper empathic understanding – 'hunches', 'intuition'
 Building bridges/helping the client connect themes
 Self-disclosure
 Confrontation
 Immediacy
 Using specific techniques from different theories

Moving on by
 Exploring and setting goals

Third-stage skills

Moving into action by
 Brainstorming
 Problem solving and decision making
 Planning and rehearsing action
 Teaching and practising skills with the client
 Evaluating

These are the skills which are usually taught as 'counselling skills' and many of them will be common to all counselling theories, some will not.

is probably the most demanding of energy and needs to be placed where energy is likely to be high. Some trainers start a session with an exercise to relax and energize and it is a good idea to follow a session by some relaxation, perhaps a coffee or meal break.

ASSEMBLE YOUR RESOURCES

You need models to teach skills – students need to see the skills in action. You may demonstrate them yourself, so it is important that you can practise what you preach. This takes courage for some people; others enjoy it. It is probably important not to be too expert so that students feel they can never reach that standard, but good enough to show the skill explicitly. Some trainers are worried that they will turn out clones if they model the skills, and this may happen in the consciously competent stage, but as students get more confident that they can do it, they usually move to their own style. Providing a range of models can prevent cloning; for example, getting other staff to demonstrate live or on video, using video material of specific skills and of some of the masters performing – Rogers, Perls and Ellis are still available on video. Audio-tapes are also useful and audio equipment is often more available. The BAC provide a good audio-visual aid catalogue.

Access to video equipment for student practice is also desirable, as it is an excellent teaching method. It provides an opportunity for the students to see themselves as others see them and to be able to study how non-verbal communication matches, or conflicts with, verbal communication and is the ideal tool for interpersonal process recall. However, it is expensive on materials, rooms and time, so you may have to compromise. Some courses use video workshops at weekends when some intensive training can be done. Audio equipment can be difficult to use if you have limited room space, but students need to have access to a tape recorder and get skilled at using it to enable them to record their work with clients.

PREPARE STUDENTS TO BE CLIENTS FOR EACH OTHER

'Fellow trainees may not constitute an appropriate source for clientele but they undoubtedly provide the best possible milieu for developing counselling skills' (Dryden and Thorne, 1991), pp. 6–7. Students must have clients to practise skills. The choices are to client for each other or to role-play. There are pros and cons for both, and you may decide to use both at different times or stages of work.

Students as clients

ADVANTAGES

- It is more real for the counsellor.
- Counsellors can experience the reality of a range of 'clients' in different stages of their lives.
- Students can use sessions to work through aspects of themselves which affect them as counsellors, e.g. prejudices, interpersonal style.
- Students get to know each other in more depth and it helps to develop a climate of trust and sharing in the group.
- The counsellor needs to be more real and caring.
- The student experiences what it feels like to sit in the client's chair.

DISADVANTAGES

- As students become better counsellors the client may go deeper, may reveal more than they intend, and because of limited time sessions, may be left in mid-air.
- Students need preparation beforehand in order to be able to share appropriate concerns at a suitable level of disclosure.
- It may conflict with work the student is doing with his or her own counsellor.

Role-play

ADVANTAGES

- Role-plays can produce specific issues to bring out the skills being practised.
- If counselling is poor, the client is not hurt.
- It gives an opportunity for the counsellor to stop and discuss tactics, e.g. in stop-start counselling.
- It gives the student an opportunity to get inside the skin of 'real' or possible clients.
- It gives participants an opportunity to display emotions in a client role with less control, and this can be helpful.
- It can be a less threatening way of introducing video – students can play 'atrocious' clients which can be fun.

DISADVANTAGES

- It is harder for the counsellor to be real and to build a relationship with a role-played client.
- Students can use role-play to prevent themselves getting involved at a personal level.

- Students can get very involved in a role, often using parts of themselves, and need an opportunity to de-role and separate themselves after the session.

USING ROLE-PLAY

If students are going to role-play clients, it is important to spend time helping them get into the role they are going to play – and helping them get out of it.

There are three methods for choosing the role:

- Provide an outline of a role and problem which the students can build on. This is useful if you want to raise specific topics to work on.
- Ask the students to think of a specific client whom they would find useful to role-play, and ask them to prepare the role beforehand.
- Ask a group of three or four students to build a client role for one of them to play, perhaps building in problems or emotions which they find difficult to work with.

To help develop the role:

- Remind the students the role is not a caricature but a 'rounded' person.
- Work briefly with the role-playing clients, asking each one questions to help them fix the role – age, family background, where they live, what they like doing, clothes, etc.
- Ask the role-players to sit quietly, close their eyes and imagine themselves in the role: sometimes confident, sometimes afraid, sometimes feeling OK, sometimes not, strong and weak.
- Ask a few more questions and then start.

De-roling is necessary at the end of the session, after the feedback:

- Give the 'clients' a few minutes to detach themselves from the role and to say out loud: 'I am not (*name*)' ..., 'I am (*name*), ... a student on this course'; 'I am similar to the role in ... ', I am different from the role in ... '.

Student preparation for being a client

It is important to make this expectation explicit in the description of the course so that students are prepared. Ask students to prepare to talk about themselves at the appropriate level, not a gut-spilling exercise, nor forced confessions, but an opportunity to look at problems or characteristics of their interpersonal style, or attitudes, assumptions or expectations which may interfere with their effectiveness as a counsellor.

I asked some trainers how they dealt with this.

Pauline said:

> I think this is a very important area of learning both for those being clients and for the trainee counsellors. I think it is important that from early on students learn to manage themselves, their feelings especially, to know when it is appropriate to stop accelerating into emotion, to be aware and be able to choose what to do with feelings. Being congruent is not letting it all hang out, it is being aware and choosing what is right for them at that moment – and being able to say so. Which doesn't mean there may not be deep feelings expressed in skills practice, but to be able to contain them at the end of the session. This is not always possible, and again there is learning in how to stay with a fellow student in an emotional state – and not to keep her in the role of client, but help her back to role of student. Being a client is only part of our lives!
>
> I find the best way to teach the client role is to model it myself being authentic, using issues from my life and being able to give clear feedback to the counsellor how I perceived her, what helped and what did not. I use 'stop-start' counselling quite a lot in training so that the client is counselled by several counsellors within a session; this means clients must be able to work with this – and give feedback how they experience the differences of the interaction with different counsellors. This is often quite subtle and leads to identifying shades of feelings.

Robert said:

> We use role play mainly but are introducing more work with each other. Students were very reluctant to use their own material at first. Some of them know each other outside as we work in quite a restricted area and they did not want to talk about their families. We have a very strong emphasis on confidentiality within the group, even to not telling anybody outside that they worked with each other. I ask them to use material which is relevant to their development as a professional counsellor, using the counselling theory they are learning to apply to themselves, or to work on values, beliefs, prejudice or oppression – when they feel oppressed and when they are aware of oppressing others. They all have personal counselling outside where they can take issues they do not want to bring to the group. Several of them are with the same counsellor and this adds another dynamic to the group – and

more learning – how to work in an incestuous environment without becoming incestuous.

Shirley said:

We use students as clients in the first term when we are revising basic skills and moving on to challenging skills, when we also use the group process to develop the challenging skills. We then use both role-play and their own material; role-play is often better for producing situations for working on the specific Gestalt and TA skills which we teach as part of our integrated course – and for helping students learn how to integrate the different models. It is also better for trying out making contracts and introducing self and counselling to different types of clients.

I work as a client occasionally, especially in the beginning when I use a group empathy exercise to find out how competent they are in the basic skills. I use it as an opportunity for the students to see me as continuing with my professional growth and learning – and as a human being who is far from perfect! (see the basic empathy exercise described as an example of 'coaching circles' in Appendix 1).

I have said above it is important that students are made aware of the commitment to being a client on the course and it is also essential that opportunities are made at the beginning of skills training to discuss the issues. Some courses give a handout with suggestions on how to be a client and what topics might be used.

TEACH FEEDBACK SKILLS

I am assuming that you are going to encourage students to give each other feedback as an important part of their learning. I have not come across a course recently where this is not done, though in the past I have found courses where the only feedback was given by the trainer, and it has only just occurred to me that my assumptions may be false. I hope not, but I have come across courses where feedback by students to each other is not well done and very unskilled. I have also met students who complain that they get very little feedback from trainers, and do not have enough confidence in the peer feedback as this is not observed by the trainer.

The BAC 'Code of Practice for Trainers in Counselling' (para. B1.7) says: 'Trainers should ensure the arrangement for initial, continuous and final assessment and feedback to trainees of their work and encourage self and peer assessment at regular intervals'.

It is important to teach feedback skills at the beginning of skills training. I think the development of good skills depends mainly on good feedback – and the development of feedback skills is an important part of counsellor training. Counsellors will need to use feedback with clients, with supervisors and, if they work in an organization, with employers and colleagues, and they will also need to use it with trainers if they are to take responsibility for their learning and for getting the education and training they need.

Feedback helps us become more aware of what we do and how we do it. Receiving it gives us an opportunity to change and modify in order to become more effective communicators. To be helpful, feedback needs to be given in a concerned and supportive way and to include both positive and negative observations. It should focus on:

- the behaviour rather than the person
  - what he does rather than what we imagine he is
  - use adverbs which relate to actions rather than adjectives which relate to qualities
- observations rather than inferences
  - what is said or done, not why (our assumptions)
- description rather than judgement
- being specific rather than generalizing
- sharing ideas and information rather than giving advice
  - personalized: 'I felt, I thought ... '
- the amount of information the receiver can use rather than the amount we would like to give
- behaviour the receiver can do something about.

When possible, sandwich negative feedback between positive, and check that the receiver hears both positive and negative. Summarizing the feedback received can be helpful, especially when it has been given by several people.

It is also necessary to explore the difficulties some students experience in talking directly to the counsellor as they give feedback – looking directly at the counsellor, and using 'you'. I think it is something in our culture which prefers to say 'she gave a good impression when she ... '. Maybe it is about being assertive and speaking from a firm centre. It is also about 'speaking from your truth'. It it struggling to put into words what you feel and think and see as accurately as possible, without the fear of seeming foolish or unkind or wrong, and at the same time being tentative, – it is as you see it at this moment, filtered through your perception.

Feedback from observers depends on accurate observation, acute listening and hearing, and being able to remember the points observed at the end of the session and select appropriately – you cannot feedback all you notice. This complete attention takes energy and students need to be able to find this energy – a self-management skill. Some courses structure their practice in triads which means there is only one observer. Others work in fours with two observers; others, in fives or sixes. Multiple observers have distinct advantages: they pick up different things, depending on the focus of their senses, and give the counsellor a wider range of feedback. They learn how differently different people experience the same stimulus; they see and experience a wider range of counsellors and of clients. The 'Gilmore' structure which Robert talked about (Chapter 3) provides a structure for this, and is detailed in Appendix 1.

Feedback from the client to the counsellor depends on inner awareness, being able to work both as a client and as an observer noting reactions. Pauline, above, emphasized how much the counsellor can learn from feedback from an aware client. The trainee as client needs to learn to monitor her feelings in the interaction and feed back to the counsellor when she felt understood and accepted or not, and when she felt the counsellor was completely congruent – or not.

Feedback to self by the counsellor needs space. Some trainers suggest the counsellor does this before hearing feedback from the client and observers, others after. I prefer it after, as the observer and client are not influenced by it, and I think it is useful for the counsellor to hear all the other feedback and save any reaction to the end. It is a very useful discipline for the counsellor to summarize all the feedback he or she hears – with reminders from the group; usually the positive is forgotten. It can also be helpful for the counsellor to get into the habit of writing it down afterwards.

Performance-specific, positive feedback with specific information concerning future improvement works better than consistently negative feedback which can be destructive and demoralizing. Consistently positive feedback can have a flavour of insincerity which may make the counsellor doubt the usefulness. Neutral feedback is not helpful – the counsellor needs to know how he or she is doing in terms of areas of competence and areas that need work.

Most difficulties that occur in the final assessment of skills are because the student has not had sufficient specific feedback during the course. Written feedback is useful at intervals to crystallize what has been learnt and what is still to be learnt (there is a form for written feedback in Appendix 2).

This preparation sounds like a lot of hard work but good preparation can help skills work to run smoothly, at least for a time. Life is often hard for the counsellor trainer! In Chapter 5 we look at building a learning group which provides the safety, support and challenge for skills learning to take place.

CHAPTER QUESTIONS

1. Do you believe it is better to teach micro-skills to students or to let them discover the skills they need by trial and error and feedback? Or would you use different methods for different skills?
2. If you teach an Integrative model, how do you select which skills are to be learnt?
3. What proportion of the timetable should be allocated to skills work?
4. Should skills sessions continue throughout the course?
5. What is your attitude towards students counselling each other in skills practice? What boundaries or ethical problems might this present?
6. What to you think about tutors demonstrating skills? About giving 'models' to students for skills?

FIVE

Building a learning group

... the success of counsellor training is intimately connected to the quality of the relationship between trainees and trainers. (Dryden and Thorne, 1991)

Developing a good learning group can be one of the hardest tasks of the trainer, and can be one of the most rewarding for trainer and trainees. This chapter aims to help you explore some of the issues around building a skills learning group in which the quality of the relationships between trainer and trainees, and trainees with each other, enhance and promote the learning. I suggest some frameworks which can help in the setting up and maintenance of such a group, give some trainer experiences of group allocation and some ideas on group contracts.

THE GROUP TASK

In a skills learning group there are two main tasks:

1. to set up, build and maintain relationships within the group to develop a climate of support and challenge for new learning;
2. to teach and provide opportunities to learn the skills.

These tasks are, of course, intertwined but they each require different skills and roles from the trainer. The first requires group skills, especially group leadership skills, and knowledge of how the dynamics of the group will affect the task of learning. It also requires the skills, attitude and ability to communicate empathy, acceptance and genuineness. The second requires not only the skills and knowledge to provide learning opportunities and teaching the skills and competencies needed, but also the skill of being an authority without being authoritative – to be able to take charge, set up structures and experiential exercises, set boundaries, assess and give feedback. We look at this latter task in Chapter 6 and explore the first task in this.

MODELS OF GROUPS

When a group comes together and interacts the behaviour of everybody is modified by the 'forces' present. The energy present can help or hinder the learning process. Building and maintaining a learning group consisting of a rich mix of individuals is a complex task and it is useful to have some frameworks to help you understand, reflect upon and work within it. You are probably aware of and use several group theories, but here is a brief look at some theories which I have found useful. These may help you clarify your own frameworks and think about group theory in relation to a group with a clear learning task.

Group Needs (TMI framework)

One framework is to be aware that when a group meets together there are three sorts of interlocking needs which have to be kept in balance:

1. *Task needs* – usually the most apparent on the surface. The need to be clear about the goal or purpose of the group and also what methods can be used to work towards the goal.
2. *Maintenance needs*. The need to develop good working relationships and a positive climate to work on the task.
3. *Individual needs*. Members have a range of needs such as to be recognized, to belong, to contribute, as well as possible individual learning needs identified in Chapter 2.

You, as trainer, may at the beginning, have to hold the responsibility to meet these needs but as the group progresses, responsibilities for meeting the needs can be shared among the members of the group. The 'task needs' highlight the importance of clarity on what is to be learnt and how; your preparation and pre-course information can stand you in good stead here. A good group contract can also help in identifying and sharing the needs.

Schutz model (developing needs)

This model suggests there are three needs which develop in sequence as the group comes together:

1. *Inclusion needs*. Each member needs to feel they belong and to work out 'who am I here?' 'who are the others here?' 'am I accepted?' 'do

I want to belong?'. This brings out the importance of helping students get to know each other as individuals early in the group, and thus the importance of devising strategies to shorten this process, and so be able to get on with the main task.

2. *Power and influence needs.* Individuals have different needs for power and influence and need to test out with each other and with the trainer where they stand. Sometimes these needs can hinder the task and require space and patience to work them through – and some restraint from the trainer at times.

3. *Affect needs.* The need to resolve liking and disliking, and being able to accept differences and decide how to work together. If you as trainer provide a good model of communicating empathy, acceptance and congruence to individuals in the group, this will encourage a facilitative climate to develop.

Tuckman's model of group movement

(Tuckman, 1965). He describes groups as progressing through four stages:

1. *Forming.* A stage of anxiety and dependence on the trainer. What is allowed and not allowed in this group? How supportive or critical will it be? What are the norms? This stage can be helped by clarifying the task and methods to reach it and by helping members communicate with, and get to know each other.

2. *Storming.* A stage of possible resistance to the trainer and to the task, and of conflict between members. Issues of power and influence are being brought out and hopefully resolved. Requires restraint from the trainer not to get involved with justifying, defending or attacking, but to use basic skills to demonstrate acceptance of the difficulties and emotions involved in this stage. Some groups take a long time to reach this stage, some reach it early, some work through easily. Attending to inclusion and maintenance needs can 'soften' it, but recognizing it as a normal stage can perhaps help you ride the storm with more equanimity.

3. *Norming.* The group begins to find ways to work together on the task and to enjoy the feelings of mutual support and feelings of making progress together.

4. *Performing.* The group can work together, can resolve conflicts and trust each other to give feedback and support in the task of learning. The energy can be very exciting at this stage and it is ideal to reach it as soon as possible. However, it is not necessarily a linear process – some groups work backwards and forwards through the stages, sometimes as the learning becomes more difficult or as individuals meet crises in their personal development, and emotions become high in the group.

Some books add a fifth stage:

5. *Mourning.* The recognition that the group is ending and of the processes it needs to go through to finish. The closer the group sometimes the harder to finish and students may be very resistant; it can be useful learning in relation to the difficulties of finishing a relationship with clients.

Bion's model of Unconscious Processes

This model (Bion, 1961) can hinder getting on with the learning task of the group. I find it can be helpful in diagnosing what is holding up the task. There are three processes which Bion calls 'basic assumptions':

1. *Dependence.* The group believes only a strong leader, a God, can protect the group from the insecurity and emotional stress of coming together. All communication goes to the leader, only his word is valid. Sometimes this is a temporary stage in the early life of the group and can be reinforced by the trainer taking too strong a lead.
2. *Pairing.* The group 'allows' the interaction to be taken over by two people and somehow believes they will produce redemption or survival for the group – others cease working.
3. *Flight/fight.* The energy of the group will be used to fight or run away; aggression or withdrawal is the norm for the group.

All these are unconscious processes which can take hold of a group, often when the task is not clear or too difficult, or there are underlying agendas hidden in the group. The best coping strategies are probably to bring the process into consciousness and help the group bring out and discuss unrecognized difficulties.

It can be useful to familiarize yourself with some of these frameworks as alternative spectacles with which to view the group, to help you decide in times of indecision 'What do I need to do next in this group?'.

GROUP ALLOCATION

If you have more than 12 students on your course you have to make decisions on group allocation. Whether you allocate or let students choose their groups depends on your purposes, philosophical framework, what learning you want to provide for the group, and how you see the task of skill training. There are pros and cons for both.

Shirley who lets students choose their groups said it was time consuming but worth the time. She said:

It puts the responsibility on to the students to think about what they want from the group, how they will get it and who they think will be most help to be with in their learning. Because there are boundaries in their choice i.e. limited number in each group, and limited time for choosing, there is usually conflict; they have to compromise their choices and recognize their power is limited. It often produces early power struggles and recognition of the need to support each other even while disagreeing. We usually spend the first session after they have chosen exploring with the small group what went on for them, what have they learnt about themselves, about other members of the group and how this relates to their counselling.

Robert, who puts the students into two groups, said:

Skills time is limited, there are other areas of the course, e.g. personal development groups, where they learn to struggle. I bring up the issue with the students and say I have divided them using criteria of gender, age, experience to get as rich a mix as possible in each group. I have had complaints from the occasional student who feels 'ordered' but most are glad not to have to choose, to get on to skills work soon and say they appreciate the challenge to work with whoever and whatever is in the group. Because the groups have to work on their own half the time they learn to take responsibility for keeping boundaries and feeling mutually responsible for each other's learning. Staff team members are sometimes sharply divided on this issue and it is important to negotiate this before each group of students arrives on the course. Some courses try different methods each year and compare results. It could be a useful piece of research.

NEGOTIATE A GROUP CONTRACT WITH THE GROUP

You are in the process of building a working alliance with the training group. The alliance contains bonds, tasks, and goals. The tasks of the group are to learn and practise the skills which need to be clearly identified. The goals are to reach a standard of competency, criteria and assessment procedures for which also need to be identified and made clear. The bonds are the relationships which need to be built between you and the students and with each other. This is helped if responsibilities of each are clarified, expectations and assumptions made explicit and open communication agreed, including opportunities for students to give feedback on your ways of working with the group. A group contract can make this explicit.

To lead into the contract the following exercise can help to make some of these explicit. In the first session, ask the students, individually or in groups of three, to write up on flip charts:

- What can I do which would help or hinder my learning?
- What could the group members do which would help or hinder my learning?
- What could the trainer(s) do which would help or hinder?

Add names. The trainer(s) should also do a similar sheet. Display the sheets, have some discussion and keep them for future review. Items from these sheets may provide issues to negotiate into a working agreement, e.g.:

- I will hinder myself by not taking any risks.
- The group can help by supporting me with gentle challenge.
- The group can help by being open and honest.
- I can help myself by asking for what I want.
- The trainers can help by being willing to demonstrate a skill.
- The trainers can hinder by not recognizing we have different learning speeds, and individual needs for acceptance.

Confidentiality

One item of importance for building trust in the group is agreement about confidentiality within the group. I find this often needs discussion and clarification – what is confidential and what are the boundaries, both among students and with trainers? It seems important to clarify that material disclosed by individuals is confidential to the people present, whether as a pair, small group or large group. Also, that skill development, successes, failures, risks taken are also not talked about outside. There is one exception to this. The BAC 'Code of Ethics for Trainers' in the section on confidentiality states:

A3.3 Trainers may not reveal confidential information concerning trainees without the permission of the trainee except in discussion:

(a) in supervision
(b) to prevent serious harm
(c) when legally required
(d) during selection, assessment, complaints etc.

I have clarified this with the BAC: it does not preclude trainers discussing students' progress in skills training, or in personal development linked to their professional development, with other trainers who are involved with teaching and assessing them. It is important that students are aware of the 'Code of Ethics for Trainers' and have opportunities for discussing items from the Code.

Other items which need to be incorporated in the group contract are:

- Commitment to giving feedback and support, to each other and to the trainer(s).
- To be cooperatively responsible for each other's learning.
- Clarification of differences between on-going evaluation and feedback and final assessments.
- Setting time to review and possibly amend the working contract.

All these help to set up a learning climate in which students can begin to feel committed to the group and to their own and each other's learning.

HELP MEMBERS TO GET TO KNOW EACH OTHER

This is often forgotten when there is a task to move into. How much needs to be done depends how much has been done in other areas of the course, but at least in the first session some activities need to be included to help members begin to know each other as individuals in this group. The exercise of forming the working agreement helps the 'knowing' and also helps the students to begin to know the trainers and vice versa.

If the members are using their own material as clients for each other they will, as they begin to practise, perhaps hear more of their inner turmoil. So it is important to share other aspects of their lives so that they can be seen as whole people. A session, or part of a session, to share and clarify individual values, beliefs, assumptions (see the discussion of value clarification (p. 61), part of Competency 5 in Chapter 6) can also deepen the interaction and make explicit some areas of possible conflict. Individuals in the group may be surprised how different they are. We often assume that because we are all 'into counselling' we have similar values and beliefs, and we may keep our differences hidden to be accepted into the group.

MONITOR THE ONGOING PROCESS OF THE GROUP WITH THE STUDENTS

I said above that the trainer needs to be aware of how the dynamics of the group will affect the learning. A trainer who takes a strong teaching/

leadership role and holds the group to the task of learning and practising skills by setting up clear structures and controlling time, while communicating empathy, respect and genuineness and helping members to get to know each other, can help, in the beginning, to produce a safe group and one that gets on with the task.

However, this often works with short courses which are set up specifically to learn basic skills. There may be power struggles with anti-authority students. Limited time may allow these to be resolved enough to move on with the task. Focusing on the task and providing clear leadership often prevents issues of power and conflict between individuals arising. The norm is to learn from the teacher, and if the teacher communicates empathically and with respect the students feel included and safe – for a time! In a diploma course of two years or more there are other dynamics affecting the skills group, and the learning of more complex skills requires a different sort of leadership after the initial weeks which will allow more interaction and more conflict. Some of the issues which may affect the group dynamic are:

- The philosophy and theoretical orientation of the course. This includes the expectations and assumptions of the relationships between staff and students, the role of the staff in managing and structuring, or not, the way other sessions of the course are managed, what responsibility students take for deciding their own learning and how they will learn.
- How the group has formed, chosen or self-chosen.
- The experience within the group of counselling. There may be a wide range of ability in skills, or a perceived range which may produce a range of feelings from 'good, I can learn from' to feelings of inferiority, envy, superiority, competition, excitement.
- The mix of individuals in the group. There may be differences in age, culture, class, gender, spiritual and other values, and educational background – a mix which produces richness to learn from, and possibly conflict as time progresses.
- The teaching/facilitating style of the trainer, and if there are co-trainers there is the dynamic between them and with the students relating to them.
- The different learning styles among the students.
- The differing rate of progress in gaining competency among the students.
- The different values and assumptions held by individual members, which become more obvious as they get to know each other.

These are issues to be aware of and possibly to explore with the students, or at least make explicit to them when difficulties arise.

So, a trainer may require one set of group skills at the beginning to form a safe group and different skills to maintain and facilitate a more interactionary group as the learning moves forward.

SKILLS AND QUALITIES A TRAINER NEEDS FOR GROUP MAINTENANCE

You need to be able to help the group explore and use the 'process' of the group, and use the learning from this to relate to their counselling. For this you need to switch from a 'teaching' role to a 'facilitating' role. How big the switch is will depend on how you play the teaching role, but it is a switch. And it will depend on your theoretical orientation how relevant the process work is to the counselling, but as much of it is about exploring interaction and communicating openly and genuinely, it would seem relevant to all counselling – clearly less to behavioural than to person-centred.

Exploring 'process' – the unspoken happenings in the group – needs courage, willingness to risk being wrong or being attacked, awareness of your inner feelings, thoughts, fantasies, emotions, awareness of what is happening in interactions between students and between individuals and yourself, decisions on what, how and when to disclose, empathy of what may be going on inside others; that is, the ability to model the skills of appropriate disclosure of yourself, of 'immediacy' and of 'advanced empathy'. These are all skills needed in counselling and are some of the most difficult skills to teach and learn. Using the group process can be an important part of skills training and the skills group an important place to model and practise them.

Mearns (1994) suggests that, in person-centred work where congruence is all important, a large group is a better forum for working on this. He suggests the small groups want to keep safe. Members develop ways of being which are acceptable to the small group to retain this safeness, and this may be a 'portrayal' of empathy and unconditional positive regard, rather than a genuine expression of themselves. He says that a large group, although more difficult, as it develops can provide opportunities and challenge leading to more congruent ways of engaging with each other, rather than the previous more guarded ways of relating. He also gives some useful ideas for 'tapping the unspoken relationship with clients' (Chapter 18), which can be helpful in the group.

Awareness of the possibility of 'portrayal' for safety could be a useful issue to raise in a small group, when the time is ripe. How to get the timing right, to risk and keep some safety is a challenge to the trainer, and to the group.

Conflict and difficulties which arise in the group give opportunities to work through and to explore the process of 'breakdown and repair' and how this may lead to new learning, and may change and deepen the interaction within the group. This is an important learning for work with clients.

Some of this process work may, of course, be done in a personal development group, but it may not be so relevant there to identify the skills as they happen, and to help the students relate this to their counselling. That depends how the task of the development group is seen. What is important is not to turn the skills group into a personal development group – to keep the main task in focus – and also not to turn it into a counselling group. A good skills learning group can be very therapeutic, but it is not a therapy group!

The group will have to end at some time, often before the end of the course and this provides opportunities to look at the skills of ending an alliance and to relate this to counselling.

This is the 'under water' work in the skills group. We move on in Chapter 6 to the clearer task of teaching and providing opportunities for the students to learn.

CHAPTER QUESTIONS

1. How much time and energy should the trainer devote to group building and maintenance in a skills training session? How much might this depend on different groups of students?
2. How much should the trainer 'manage' the group, how much leave to the students? Should this be tutor choice or course policy?
3. Is skills learning facilitated by students choosing their own groups or tutors?
4. Is a group learning contract useful and worth the time taken setting it up?
5. If so, what might a contract usefully contain?
6. Is skills learning facilitated by spending time exploring the 'process' of the group?
7. What do you consider is an ideal relationship between a trainer and trainees when assessment is involved?

SIX
Teaching the skills and competencies

In the previous chapters we looked at all the preparations which need to be done to set up skills training; in this chapter I will set out a framework for teaching skills, then some further ideas for teaching the skills related to the competencies identified in Chapter 1, and explore some of the issues arising.

The purpose of skills training is to enable trainees:

- To discriminate between helpful and unhelpful ways of responding to clients.
- To make helpful responses in a clear and effective manner.
- To be able to integrate and use the skills flexibly in counselling sessions.

A FRAMEWORK FOR TEACHING SKILLS

Taking into account fears of producing technicians rather than counsellors, the micro-skills approach has been demonstrated as a good way of improving communication and interpersonal skills and of relearning ways that are helpful and respectful to clients rather than unhelpful or damaging. Below I outline a framework for teaching micro-skills.

This approach entails learning one skill at a time, and for each skill, being able to discriminate between accurate and inaccurate understanding of what the client is communicating, and to be able to make helpful, and not make unhelpful, responses to this communication.

There are five stages to the teaching: **instruction, modelling, practice, feedback,** and **integrating and generalizing**.

Instruction

- First giving an overall model and rationale to trainees incorporating the skills to be learnt in this part of the training, to tie up with the theory and philosophy of the course; developing a cognitive understanding.
- Instruction in the specific skills to be learnt, including their purpose, when and where they can be used or not used, and giving time for discussion and clarification.
- Instruction in feedback skills is important at this point, to highlight the necessity for trainees to learn how to do them well in order to help each other learn.

Handouts and/or suitable reading and references can be given to back up the instruction.

Modelling

- Providing models of discrimination, i.e. setting up client statements, perhaps on video or audio, with accurate and inaccurate descriptions of the content and emotions which are being communicated.
- Providing models of helpful responses to client statements which illustrate the skill to be learnt, and possibly providing unhelpful responses. Also providing models of part or whole counselling sessions to show appropriate use of the skill and if necessary finding ways of 'highlighting' the specific skill so that it stands out for the trainees.
- Providing models of giving both positive and negative feedback and the skills needed, and the skills of receiving feedback and reflecting upon it.

There is some disagreement whether 'bad' models help learning. I think they often provide light relief for some of the intensity which can accompany skills training and they undoubtedly raise energy in discussion. Some trainers are worried that models will turn out clones and prefer to skip this stage, to move into practice and shape the skill by feedback. Bandura (1969) said that most human behaviour is learned through observation of models, and I believe that people learn more easily this way. The models need to be good, but not too good to make the trainee think 'I could never do that'. I also believe it is very important for trainers to demonstrate, and here it is useful to co-train so that one of you can be the client. The co-trainer will more likely know the level and substance of what is needed to be brought as client, and also provide a model of how to be a client. You may, however, need to use trainees as clients, and it is important that they have prepared for this (see Chapter 4) and the trainer demonstrator takes care not to over-expose the trainee, especially in a large group. Using trainees as clients can cause complications and overshadow the skill being demonstrated, but it can be excellent learning for them, to have the experience of working with a skilled counsellor.

Video or audio-tape models are very useful, both made by the trainers and by others, including the masters – Rogers, Perls and Ellis (see BAC AVA Catalogue 1995). They can be stopped and specific use of skills discussed. Videos and audio-tapes which trainees can use out of session are helpful, especially if the particular skills are 'highlighted' in some way on the video or audio-tape.

Live or video demonstration gives a rounder view of the skill; what is important is hearing and seeing when possible, several ways of using the skill. If you use video or audio of whole or part counselling sessions, it is important to have some way of identifying the particular skill which is being learnt. To supplement live models, written models can also be used, including transcripts of counselling sessions for the students to identify the skills they are learning. There is a useful book *Exercises in Helping Skills* developed by Egan (1994) to go with his *Skilled Helper* (1994) which gives statements from clients for counsellors to practise identifying the content and emotions.

Finally, there is the effect the trainer has as a model generally. Connor (1994) commenting on research on effects of modelling, and lack of research in this area, states:

> Perhaps the most challenging aspect of the theory surrounding the effectiveness of modelling concerns the function of the trainer as a model, not just on video tapes of specific skills but in the total process of training. ... variations in the way in which the trainer is perceived by trainees could have a profound effect upon the outcomes of specific skills. It is surprising that ... there is not the realisation that there is a 'macro' modelling effect as well as the 'micro' effect from the trainer. The total training process is a model which is more than the sum of the component parts of the training. (p. 149)

This seems an important thought to reflect upon and notice in our work.

Practice

Practice can take two main forms. First exercises and activities give brief practice in the skill being learnt (see, for example, the basic empathy exercise described under 'coaching circles' in Appendix 1). There are numerous resource books for this – see Inskipp (1993) and Dainow and Bailey (1988).

Second, in counselling practice, trainees use each other as clients, either using their own material or role-playing, and focus on the skill to be learnt. Trainees can work in twos, giving feedback to each other supplemented by the trainer, or threes, taking it in turns to be counsellor, client and observer, or in fours, as above, adding another observer or a manager who keeps time and structure and, if necessary, works any equipment (useful if video or audio is used). The 'Gilmore' structure (up to six in a group) set out in Appendix 1 is used by many trainers; it has a very clear structure for working and for feedback, which trainees can learn to manage on their own with the trainer coming in at intervals to give feedback. The 'goldfish bowl' – a pair working within a larger group – is also used by many trainers. This can mean a long time before everybody has had a turn to practise, although the structure can provide good learning on the way and the trainer sees all 'performers'.

Feedback

This is probably the most important part of the process. Without good feedback, skills practice is often wasted, indeed the trainees may decrease in skill. It needs good management to ensure that each trainee is given regular feedback by the trainer, as well as by peers, and that self-evaluation is encouraged as part of learning to be a 'reflective counsellor'. It is also important for the trainer to recognize that some trainees become over anxious when the trainer is present, however facilitative and empathic. The exploration of these anxieties can be an important part of personal development and can be explored in the skills group, in personal tutorials or in personal development groups, or can be used as 'client work' in practice groups. This exploration as client can often provide good practice for the more difficult second-stage skills.

Good feedback by the trainer, and teaching the feedback skills to the trainees at the beginning of skills training, can pay high dividends in skills development. Feedback is discussed in detail in Chapter 4 as part of Preparation.

Integrating and generalizing the skills to work with clients

In this section I emphasize the importance of breaking down the skills and practising them separately, but, as mentioned above, this has dangers. Trainees may learn to produce mechanical responses to clients rather than authentic empathic responses. Rogers (1980) called this 'the appalling consequences' (p.139) of the exciting work he had initiated by analysing audio-recordings and identifying responses which 'turned a client's dull and desultory talk into a focused self-exploration' (p.138). He was shocked by the distortions and caricatures which came from an over emphasis on skilled responses, and which ignored the real communication of empathy by authentic, caring counsellors.

There is an apt reminder from Wordsworth's '*The Tables Turned*':

> Our meddling intellect
> Misshapes the beauteous form of things
> We murder to dissect.

These micro-skills then need to be integrated by trainees into work with clients on their real concerns. It can be seen as trainees reaching the stage of unconscious competence in 'communication and interpersonal skills' and building these into their own personal style of relating to clients.

These issues need to be explored in the skills group and carried over into supervision and into theory sessions; this probably means good liaison between staff to complement each other's work.

ASSESSMENT AND EVALUATION

It is very important to separate assessment from evaluative feedback and for the trainees to be very clear which is which. You, or the trainees, may want on-going assessments of their skills, rather than a final assessment at the end of the course. If so, clear structures need to be set up and records kept so that cumulative assessments form part of the final qualification. We look at this in more detail in Chapter 7 on assessment.

Consistent use of the five-stage framework takes time and energy but is vital in building good basic skills as the groundwork for good counselling, and for developing the more advanced skills.

I will now go on to look at the skills contained within the competencies listed in Table 1.1, and give some brief ideas of how those might be taught and learnt.

COMPETENCY 1. MEET AND CONTRACT WITH THE CLIENT

The skills and tasks involved in the following four areas are explored:

- Client assessment skills.
- Introduce self and counselling.
- Negotiating a working agreement. Introduce and agree audio-recording if applicable.
- Begin to build a working relationship.

These four areas obviously overlap with each other, but for the purpose of looking at how the skills are taught it is useful to explore them as separate entities.

Client assessment skills

There is a difference of opinion as to whether trainees need these skills. If the trainees are working in a placement where assessment of clients is done before allocation to a trainee they will not need them there. However, at some time they may not have this service, and in many placements no assessment is done, so trainees need these skills if they are to work ethically, i.e. not beyond their competence, and with some idea of the client's readiness and commitment to counselling.

Skills:

- First stage skills, and asking for and giving information.
- Form-filling with the client.
- Skills of observation, self-awareness of body, senses, emotions, thoughts, fantasies. What is being picked up from the client.
- Relating awareness to known theory and own competence.

How do different courses teach these skills?

Brian who works in a counselling agency, said:

> Trainees do not learn these skills, as clients are assessed by an experienced counsellor and then allocated to students. Students are not allowed to take clients other than from the Agency. The Agency runs brief assessment training for counsellors who have been with the Agency for two years. The students have a session on how to recognize psycho-pathology in clients and do some role-play on how to say they cannot work with a client. This is tied up with how to refer the client, probably to a more experienced counsellor in the Agency. This is taught as part of the theory course and the skills are practised there in the large group.

Pauline, who works in a university, said:

> We do not encourage students to do assessments in the formal sense but give them some guidelines on 'when not to take a client' in theory sessions. Students must check with their supervisor after a first session with a client and they then discuss if there might be difficulties. The IPR work we do with the students would help them in their own awareness in being able to answer: What is my discomfort with this client – is it enough for me to decide not to work with them?

Shirley, who works in a college said:

We give the students a form to obtain information from the client at a first interview. They discuss the form in their skills group, alter if they wish, and then practise using the form in role-plays. We give an outline of client role-plays so that they get a range of clients. With the form is a handout giving guidelines when not to agree to take a client on, which we discuss and relate to some work on psycho-pathology. They have some role-play practice in saying 'No' to a client and referring on. We do not relate self-awareness skills specifically to this, but we could help students look for and identify these in the role-plays.

Introduce self and counselling

Skills:

- First stage skills, and selecting and giving appropriate information for individual clients.

Few courses seem to teach this specifically, it 'comes up' in supervision and is talked about, but not often actually practised with feedback. I think it is important that trainees are skilled in being able to explain counselling to clients, to say something of how they will work together, what they expect from the client and how that might help. Judging the right depth of explanation for each client is a skill, as well as being able to explain briefly, and at the same time, begin to build the alliance. The point in the course where trainees begin to see clients may be a time of chaotic thinking and feeling for trainees as they are exposed to new theories, new feelings and a shake-up of values and attitudes – a good learning place, but they need some ordering of thoughts about counselling to pass on to clients. Some skills training in this is therefore relevant.

A lot of criticism of counsellors by clients seems to stem from the client not understanding what the counsellor is doing, not being sure what they are expected to do and not understanding how what is happening can help them. Some agencies, and some individual freelance counsellors, provide a leaflet which clarifies these points for the client – producing this could be another skill – but it is still useful to discuss and clarify these potential misunderstandings with the client in the first session.

The following describes the different approaches of two courses to teaching these skills. One course uses role-played clients in the skills group and does a lot of work on identifying the different feelings counsellors have with different clients when they first meet them, identifying what criteria they use to decide how much to tell the client about themselves and about counselling. They use a brief form of IPR on some of the role-played sessions to explore the amount of information that they are picking up in the first interaction, of which they are not immediately aware. The trainees are encouraged to begin to create a framework for the counselling process by clarifying roles and expectations, and possibly defining object-ives and time-scales. The objective is to make the process as transparent as possible, opening up channels of communication based on equality.

The other course sets written work on these skills, asking the students to write out what they might say about themselves and how they might explain counselling to the client. These are then read out in small groups and discussed, then one from each group role-plays their presentation to the whole group.

Negotiating a working agreement

Skills:

- First-stage skills, and purpose and preference stating appropriate self-disclosure, information giving.

Some courses do not teach this explicitly and do not expect trainees to make contracts with clients, but the following is an extract from the BAC 'Code of Ethics for Counsellors':

Contracting

2.2.10 Clear contracting enhances and shows respect for the client's autonomy.

2.2.11 Counsellors are responsible for communicating the terms on which counselling is being offered, including availability, the degree of confidentiality offered, and their expectations of clients regarding fees, cancelled appointments and any other significant matters. The communication of terms and any negotiations over these should be concluded before the client incurs any financial liability.

2.2.12 It is the client's choice whether or not to participate in counselling. Reasonable steps should be taken in the course of the counselling relationship to ensure that the client is given an opportunity to review the terms on which counselling is being offered and the methods of counselling being used.

Other codes of ethics also include guidance on contracting.

Clear contracting requires good interpersonal skills to communicate empathy, acceptance and congruence, at the same time as giving and receiving information, beginning to build a relationship and negotiating the boundaries of working together. It needs ability in timing and pacing the interaction and in being able to judge how much needs to be negotiated at this point – a client in crisis and in great emotional distress may not have much free energy to hear any terms of contract. However, not conveying minimal information to the client in the early stages may cause difficulties. Here is an example of this. A trainee was on a training course where she had to check with her supervisor after the first session as to whether it was appropriate for her to work with a client. She had a client in great distress who talked non-stop for two sessions disclosing some serious abuse. When the trainee eventually got a word in to say she might not be able to go on working with her the client was very angry and aggressive towards the trainee.

Appropriate skills for interrupting the flow, coping with strong emotions and ensuring the client hears important information at the outset are difficult to master, especially for person-centred trainees. It has been usual practice not to teach the 'challenge' skills until trainees have mastered the first-stage skills, though Egan (1994) now includes challenge skills in his new first stage.

This is an issue which may differentiate teaching 'counselling skills' from teaching 'counsellor skills'. The Differentiation Project (Russell *et al.*, 1992) quoted in Chapter 1 identified a specific role of counsellor which 'is clearly and explicitly contracted, and the boundaries of the relationship identified'. If trainees need to learn to contract and set up these boundaries, they may need some challenging skills to cope with difficulties such as the example above.

Below are four examples from different courses of how contracting can be dealt with:

We encourage students to make brief agreements with each other in their counselling skills practice, even for one short session. We also set up role-plays for students to negotiate agreements for both short- and long-term work. We require them to use tape-recording with clients from the beginning and they role-play negotiating this, getting a form of agreement signed by the client, and setting up the equipment. We think this helps the students to be more confident in asking the client for permission. We have found it is often the counsellor who is more frightened of the recorder than the client.

We teach this in Professional Practice, rather than in a skills group. The students spend time in threes sorting out what they would want in an agreement. They then build a client profile for one of them to role-play. They join with another three and work out the role-plays across the group. In this way they experience and try out different ways of working.

We are very insistent on students making very clear contracts with clients, and of re-negotiating them regularly. We practise these in supervision groups, often when a student is starting with a new client, and also practise the re-negotiating as the sessions progress. Our students do a lot of short-term work which makes good contracting essential.

We have not taught this specifically, it comes up in supervision and is discussed then, but no skills practice is done. Maybe we should think about including this in skills work.

You can see from this that different courses include this work in different sections of the course; it might be taught and practised in the skills group, explored in theory sessions and assessed in supervision and in this case may need some integration by the staff.

Dryden and Feltham (1992) give very clear and useful ideas on assessment, introduction and contracting.

Beginning to build a working relationship

Skills:

- First stage skills – the ability to communicate empathy, acceptance and genuineness at a basic level.
- Self-awareness skills, awareness of the client and ability to judge what degree of warmth and openness may be appropriate for this client.

Skilful assessment, introduction and contracting will begin to build the relationship. There is some evidence that counsellors who work well in short-term work have the ability to build a relationship rapidly, and this may be connected to the counsellor being perceived as 'attractive' by the client. Social influence theory (Strong, 1968) suggests that when clients perceive the counsellor as expert, attractive and trustworthy they are more willing to get involved in the helping process – therefore it is useful for counsellors to enhance this perception. Increasing the ability to communicate the core qualities is one way of enhancing this perception, at the same time as not over-developing the 'expert' role.

Using Interpersonal Process Recall with audio-tapes of first or second sessions with clients, can help trainees to develop their skills of awareness of themselves, the client, and the process going on between them. It can help them explore why they find it easier to build rapport with some clients and how they manage themselves and their emotions when beginning with clients.

COMPETENCY 2. DEVELOP, MAINTAIN AND END A COUNSELLING RELATIONSHIP

(The importance and the depth of the relationship depends on the theory and the duration of counselling.)

The following skills and tasks are involved in this competency:

1. Communicate empathy, respect and genuineness.

   • First-stage skills.
   • Self-awareness and developing authenticity.
   • Second-stage skills of deeper empathy, self-disclosure, immediacy.
   • Judging when to withhold empathy and still communicate respect.

2. Review, repair if necessary.

   • Skills as above and 'process' awareness.
   • Confrontation and 'immediacy' – identify and communicate what is happening in the interaction with the client.

3. Recognize/make explicit/work with transference and counter-transference.

   • Skills as above.
   • Ability to communicate the awareness to the client appropriately.
   • Skills of working with the client using specific counselling theory.
   • Keeping appropriate boundaries.

4. End the relationship.

   • Skills as above.
   • Knowing when, and how, to begin terminating.
   • Keeping the client aware of ending in brief counselling.
   • Setting up appropriate structures to enable the client to leave the process as cleanly as possible, e.g. reviewing skills.
   • Developing creative finishing skills.
   • Coping with client's, and own, feelings of loss (sometimes).

Most of the above skills are listed in Table 4.1, especially as second-stage skills. In addition are the self-awareness and self-management skills which we will come to later. Work on transference and counter-transference will depend on your theory base, but recognition of this will depend on self-awareness. Ability to explore this with the client (if you want to) will depend on good skills of empathy, 'immediacy', self-disclosure and confrontation.

It is these second-stage skills which are more challenging for the client – and for the counsellor – which are more difficult to teach and learn; it is noticeable there are fewer exercises and activities published for practising these. This is partly because it is easier to practise first-stage skills in short counselling sessions with a new client; opportunities to practise second-stage skills usually require longer sessions and a more established relationship.

These second-stage skills need to be presented and modelled as in the framework, and opportunities for practice could be:

(a) by setting up role-plays for clients which require the counsellor to use the specific skills;
(b) by pairing trainees to work with each other in counselling over several sessions so that the work deepens;
(c) by encouraging trainees to use and identify the skills in group situations – skills group, personal development group and large group, and to record and reflect on the use by themselves or others, in their learning journals;
(d) by IPR training with video or audio-tape, using counselling sessions with other trainees, or using audio-tapes from 'real' clients;
(e) by using 'coaching circles' (see Appendix 1), either with a role-played client or with a co-trainer role-playing or being a real client;
(f) in supervision, by role-plays of client situations, or by asking trainees to bring audio-tapes which illustrate their use of the particular skill.

An example of how one course uses (b) above, pairing of trainees, is the following:

> The trainees counsel each other in pairs for one term with some staff live observation, and with sessions written up particularly noting skills used. This means the trainees work in more depth, and there is more to explore in the relationship, than in doing occasional short sessions with each other. This enables them to have more practice in the second- and third-stage skills, and in the particular theory skills of the course. Trainees are required to practise writing up casenotes on each session, trying out different frameworks for the notes, so that they have some experience before working with 'real' clients.

Finding ways for trainees to learn these skills is a challenge for trainers, the modelling of them by the trainer when opportunities arise – e.g. 'group storming' – provides some of the best learning. I have found IPR is one of the best methods for learning to use the skills; it can give opportunities to try out putting difficult things into words in a safe situation. It is also good for developing 'process' and physical sensory awareness. There are some useful ideas also in Mearns (1994), chapter 17.

COMPETENCY 3. WORK IN A SESSION

Purpose:

- to empower the client and enable him or her to explore and work on concerns and issues – and leave.

Skills:

- Communication and interpersonal skills from all three stages.
- Specific skills from specific theories.
- Skills to
  (a) integrate the micro-skills into authentic responses;
  (b) choose which skills at each point in the session;
  (c) operate within professional codes;
  (d) use the relationship and interaction appropriately;
  (e) monitor progress, review and recontract if necessary;
  (f) pace the session and bring to a close.

Integrate the skills

I have already mentioned the importance of this at the end of the skills framework. Becoming competent in working in a session with a client is the purpose of the whole of the skills training. Theory discussion, modelling and practice need setting up to show trainees how to do this, and to help them develop their individual style of working. To be authentic, not pseudo-empathic.

Choose which skills

The overall skill the trainee needs is the ability to make choices of the skills he has, and use them appropriately. Probably the only way to help this learning is to use lots of examples of counselling sessions, or extracts from sessions, preferably on video or audio, though written examples are also useful, and to help the trainee identify what choices are made. In this way trainees can become aware of intention – how the theoretical backing enables the counsellor to work with purpose. Your skill may be in finding examples specifically for your course and developing your own, or in helping the trainees develop them. Experiential work in theory sessions can provide good practice of these skills. This work on the skill of 'choosing' will obviously overlap with supervision and with theory work and maybe it is important for staff (if they are different from the skills trainers) to co-ordinate work with all three sections.

Operate within professional codes

This will tie up with exploring and discussing the codes of ethics and practice for both counsellors and for trainers. The skills content of this is developing awareness of values and the skills of self-awareness and self-management. There is also the skill of ethical problem solving. This skill is set out in detail in Bond (1993) and incorporates six steps:

1. Produce a brief description of the problem or dilemma.
2. Whose dilemma is it anyway – client, counsellor or shared?
3. Consider all available ethical principles and guidelines.
4. Identify all possible courses of action.
5. Select the best course of action.
6. Evaluate the outcome.

Bond suggests that counsellors can become more skilled in this process by training. He gives some examples to work through and it could be useful for trainers to produce examples, or to use issues as they arise to give trainees practice in this skill.

Use the relationship and interaction appropriately

I have explored this in the last section. Using 'appropriately' in the session is the skill of choosing sensitively when to be 'immediate', when to disclose thoughts, feelings, fantasies or personal experience. Models can be provided by examples of good, or bad, use in sessions on video, audio or in written transcripts, and practice can be monitored in supervision, or in role-played sessions.

Monitor progress, review and recontract if necessary

To be competent at this seems to require the trainee to be purposeful and intentional within the session. To empower the client by exploring with him or her how the work is going and how to proceed – a joint enquiry, not the expert curing the patient. McNamee and Gergen (1992) discussing the dangers of 'professionalism' state that:

> In a free society women, as well as men, must have access to the thinking of the persons they consult in order to prevent 'professionals disguised as experts' from making their choices for them. (p. 22)

This seems to require the skill of being open and encouraging feedback from the client, being flexible in using theory and being able to explain it in lay terms, willing to admit being wrong, and assertive in holding ground when necessary. Trainer modelling is perhaps the best way of teaching this!

Pace the session and bring to a close

This needs skills to hold boundaries of time (often difficult for trainees), to help the client to focus, to recognize how much time specific techniques may need, e.g. using guided imagery with a client needs plenty of time to bring him or her back to the session and 'ground' the work; skills to hold or break silence, to slow the pace for emotions to emerge, to quicken or energize when necessary, to stay with 'stuckness' if it is useful; to find ways to end sessions which accord with the theory worked with, e.g. some give homework, some summarize or get the client to summarize, some like to finish with hope, some like to finish with unfinished issues – the skill of choosing, again with 'intention'.

Working in the session with a client is what all our training is about. This section has explored only some of the wide range of skills needed. Being skilled and competent at it is a life-long learning task in which, at its best, creativity and artistry flow into the interaction and client and counsellor are changed for the better, for themselves and for the society they live in.

To be a creative, artistic counsellor depends on developing all our senses, becoming a 'tuned instrument' able to resonate, and able to use this information to orchestrate body, mind and emotions in duet with the client.

The next section looks at the skills of developing this awareness.

COMPETENCY 4. DEVELOP SELF-AWARENESS SKILLS WITHIN THE COUNSELLING SESSION

Purpose:

- to differentiate own internal world from that of the client;
- to use own internal awareness to further the work with the client;
- to develop awareness of how differences in culture, race, age, etc. may affect the interaction with the client.

Skills:

- Develop self-scanning skills.
- Sort sensations and communicate appropriately.
- Develop awareness of 'process'.
- Communicate awareness appropriately.

Developing the 'person' of the counsellor is an aim for all training courses. The importance placed on this and the depth of development is determined by the theoretical and philosophical background of the course.

Most courses allocate special sessions for 'personal development' and many now insist the trainees have personal counselling during the course. All this will feed in to the development of this competency, but, from my explorations with several trainers, I think there could be some learning and practice of specific skills to help trainees incorporate their personal development learning into their work with clients. How this might be carried out is discussed in the following sections.

Self-scanning skills

The skills framework could be used to teach trainees how to scan themselves for bodily sensations, emotions, thoughts, fantasies, pictures in the mind and to build this in to their way of working. I find many people are out of touch with their bodies and cannot use the physical sensations which could alert them to what is happening in the session, and possibly to counter-transference. This can be taught and practised, as can scanning for emotions, thoughts etc. Some Gestalt exercises are good for this; Passons (1975), Chapter 4, is a useful source. Skill at this scanning can open a rich field of knowledge for the trainee, about themselves and about themselves in interaction.

Sort sensations and communicate them appropriately

It needs skill to use this rich knowledge. Again I find IPR training is the best source for this learning. The IPR workshop in Appendix 1 will give you some ideas.

Modelling and practice in these skills can also be encouraged in group work within the course. It is often helpful if skills can be named and identified in these groups so that trainees develop a vocabulary to be able to reflect on and monitor them for their self-assessment.

Develop awareness of interaction process and communicate appropriately

These skills are some of the hardest for trainees to develop. 'Process' can be an intangible concept, hard to describe, model and teach. The theoretical background determines its importance for work with clients, but an awareness of how the trainee is perceiving and being perceived by the client, and the ability to put this into words when necessary, is basic to developing an open and fruitful working alliance.

IPR again seems the most useful learning tool. A demonstration by the trainer using IPR with a video replay of a counselling session, can be a good way of looking at the skills of identifying and exploring the process of a session.

Encouraging trainees to record in case notes their awareness of themselves and the interaction process also helps to develop these skills, and an emphasis on this in supervision is further reinforcement.

Awareness of how interaction between counsellor and client is influenced by differences in culture, race, age etc. overlaps with skills of the next section.

COMPETENCY 5. MANAGE SELF

Purpose:

- to enable trainees to work ethically and authentically with a wide range of clients;
- to help them manage their resources to live and work optimally.

Skills:

- Clarify own values, beliefs, attitudes and ethics.
- Manage own physical, mental, emotional and spiritual life.
- Commit self to continued professional development.

Gilmore (1973) has said that 'acceptance in counselling is the celebration of diversity and complexity in others'. We can only celebrate diversity if we are clear about our own values and attitudes, and are open to widening our experiences of life and the variety of ways in which it is lived. Egan (1994) suggests counsellors need to model healthy living, extending themselves physically, mentally, emotionally and spiritually. Can we, or should we, help trainees develop healthy living skills? Counselling can be a very stressful occupation and if a trainee develops skills to live as zestfully as possible he or she will leave the course better equipped to cope with the stresses.

Training could include exercises on value clarification (Kirschenbaum, 1977), activities to increase acceptance of a wider range of people, or seeking new experiences, new roles, trying out expression in different media – painting, singing, dancing, claywork, (examples in Gilmore, 1973). This is an opportunity to include training in working in a multi-cultural, multi-ethnic society and with individuals with special needs. Egan and Cowan (1979) suggest seven 'packages of skills that aid personal and social development'. Trainees could be encouraged to find and share creative ways of extending their living skills and their desire to go on learning, so developing their personal and professional self. Much of this might be included in personal development groups, rather than in skills groups, and could, perhaps, give more professional purpose to this part of the course. An issue for debate.

COMPETENCY 6. REFLECTING, RECORDING, MONITORING, USING SUPERVISION

Purpose:

- to develop a 'reflective practitioner';
- to encourage effective and responsible use of supervision.

Skills:

- Devise and use methods for reflecting on and recording work with clients.
- Ability to prepare for, present and use learning from supervision, including ability to make a supervision contract.

The main thrust of my work in the last few years has been in developing work in supervision, and one of the important issues has been to recognize the part the supervisee plays in effective supervision. If it is to be a 'passionate joint enquiry' (John Rowan, verbal comment in workshop), the supervisee needs skills to take some responsibility. These skills are set out in detail by Inskipp and Proctor (1988, 1994). Here I will suggest some headings.

Skills for reflecting and recording

Reflecting: developing ability and motivation

- to develop an internal 'fair witness' who can stand back and look in on the work without criticizing;
- to commit time and effort to this;
- to practise using IPR.

Recording: developing ability and motivation

- to devise systems of recording which work for the individual and use them;
- to be aware of ethical and legal issues.

Skills for using supervision

Preparing: reflecting, monitoring, deciding what to bring
Presenting: devising ways to present, efficiently, creatively

Using: skills to identify and ask for needed learning;
             skills to give feedback on what is helpful, or not;

skills to build the learning into the counselling;
skills to give feedback and learn from others in group
supervision.

More courses are beginning to teach supervision skills before the trainees
start supervision and trainees are finding this very useful, especially in
realizing that they can take responsibility for developing the supervision so
that it enhances their own learning.

COMPETENCY 7. DEVELOP REFERRAL PROCEDURES

Purposes:

- to ensure safety of the client;
- to work within ethical boundaries;
- to develop efficient and helpful referral procedures.

Skills:

- Know own limits of competence;
- Develop referral resources;
- Negotiate referral with a client;
- Receive referrals appropriately.

Know own limits of competence.

This is tied up with the ability to assess clients which we explored
in Competency 1. It is also the ability of the trainees to do a realistic
self-assessment of their stage of professional development, emotional and
physical resources, personal support and present commitment. This
requires skills of self-exploration and self-challenge, the ability to use
supervision, to have clear ethical values, and to know what they do not
know. As trainer your challenge is to help the trainees build these skills
into their ongoing work so that the skills are a continual part of their
professional and personal development. Again, this skills work may be
part of personal counselling or personal development groups, and will
overlap with theory and supervision work.

Develop referral resources

This requires skills of searching, making contact, keeping records, building
a network of professional contacts. If the trainee is working within an
agency, it requires the ability to clarify the agency's referral procedures –
asking the right questions in the right way.

Negotiate referral with a client

This requires the skills of referring without rejecting, and without making the client feel he or she is too ill or too difficult. It may also require the skill of saying 'No' and keeping boundaries.

These skills can be modelled and practised using role-plays.

Receive referrals appropriately

This can be the skills of deciding what information is needed when a client is referred, how to refuse unwanted information, checking what, if anything, the person referring wants from the counsellor.

For trainees working in an agency, e.g. a doctor's practice, it may be the skills of negotiating what sort of patients/clients will be referred, skills of clarifying expectations of what counselling can and cannot do.

The skills of receiving referrals by telephone – and producing the right answer-phone response – can also be worth practising. Again, all the above skills can be demonstrated and then practised using role-play.

COMPETENCY 8. WORK IN AN ORGANIZATION/AGENCY

Purposes:

- to work ethically with clarification of role, tasks, responsibilities and boundaries.

Skills:

- Negotiate a clear and comprehensive contract.
- Group skills as a team member.
- Sharing information appropriately.

All the communication and interpersonal skills are obviously needed, and the contracting skills mentioned in Competency 1. There is also the ability to know when to be assertive and when to be compliant, and the skills to communicate this. The complex issues which may arise in this work could be used to set up role-plays to rehearse and practise the skills needed.

The BAC Courses Recognition Group are in the process of publishing a paper setting out 'Guidelines for client work and supervision in recognized courses', which raises some of these complex issues. By the time this book is published the paper will probably be available from the BAC.

COMPETENCY 9. WORK AS A FREELANCE COUNSELLOR

Purpose:

- to work ethically and legally as a counsellor in private practice.

Skills:

- Set up suitable accommodation.
- Publicize self and the service.
- Use business skills, keep accounts, tax returns.
- Set up support and accountability.

Some training courses do not allow trainees to work freelance before they are qualified, and there is some dispute on this and how long they should wait after qualification. However, some trainees do work freelance, and many may at some time after leaving a course, so it is important that the skills for this work are brought into a course at some point.

There is an excellent book recently published (McMahon, 1994, *Setting up your own private practice*) which covers all the skills and tasks for working in an ethical and business-like way.

This is rather a marathon chapter and covers a much wider range of skills than are usually considered in skills training. You may rightly decide that I have included more tasks than skills, but I hope in listing the competencies I have raised issues for discussion – should this be in the curriculum, where, who should teach it. How much can the trainees take responsibility for ensuring they have all these competencies to an 'acceptable level' when they leave the course?

The issue of 'acceptable level' is still unresolved, but I raise it again in Chapter 7 on assessment.

CHAPTER QUESTIONS

1. How do you help trainees integrate learned micro-skills into work with clients?
2. What are the disadvantages of modelling skills for trainees?
3. How do you separate evaluation of on-going work from assessment for qualification?
4. As a skills trainer, how do you liaise with supervisors to help trainees integrate skills work with client work?
5. How do you allocate the different Competencies 1–9 across the curriculum?
6. Should self-management skills be practised in personal development groups?
7. Should preparation for supervision be part of skills work or part of supervision?
8. How responsible should a trainer be for ensuring trainees have skills to work in private practice?

SEVEN
Assessment

In this chapter I explore issues of assessment and power; the two purposes of assessment; structures of assessment and how these need to match with the theory and philosophy of counselling, and with the course; the reliability and validity of skills assessment; the issues of on-going and final assessment; how skills assessment fits in with the whole assessment process and with the assessment of competencies; who should assess, what to assess, and the criteria needed.

POWER AND JUDGEMENT

You, as trainer, are a gatekeeper to the profession of counselling. You are accountable and have an ethical responsibility to clients, to the profession, to the trainees and to the public generally for your judgement, or your share in the judgement, on this trainee. Has the trainee reached a stage of competence where he or she can be certified to the public as a reflective, competent counsellor who will help, not harm, clients – and who is committed to on-going personal and professional development?

This is a powerful and responsible position. How do you exercise this power, and how do you equate this with your values and attitudes about counselling, about power and judgement, and about empowering trainees? You can share this power and responsibility with trainees by structuring the course so that trainees assess themselves and each other for all or part of the course; there are examples of this later in the chapter. It is perhaps useful to ask whether we can ever lose the responsibility of gatekeeper completely. Are you finally responsible for setting the standards, however much negotiated? Does your knowledge and experience and role of trainer give you power and responsibility which cannot all be shared with trainees?

I find that this is a difficult area for many trainers. The closer they work in a 'facilitator' role as trainer, the harder it is for them to accept the role of 'judge'. Some say 'we never fail a trainee, only defer until they are ready'; this assumes that any trainee selected for the course has the potential to become a counsellor – and this may not be true. It may not be of good service to a trainee to let him or her go on trying, because to fail is to fail as a person. Continuous clear feedback during the course can help trainees accept, and choose, that the role of counsellor is not for them. Failing a trainee is hard for trainers, especially those who really prefer the counsellor role, who see possible potential and fear that failure may harm the trainee. The trainer has to face the ethical responsibility to clients and the profession who are at a distance, while the vulnerable trainee is close at hand. Dryden and Feltham (1994), writing on assessment, emphasize that:

> Trainees should enter a course knowing that formal assessment is an integral part of it, with a consequence being the possibility of failure. Do not convey any vague or ambiguous messages about the ease or probability of passing the course.

A hard message but stressing the need for integrity and honesty.

The importance of this 'gatekeeper role' highlights the need for good support and supervision for the trainer, and for the team of trainers who need to support and challenge each other on these difficult decisions.

PURPOSES OF ASSESSMENT

The ethical responsibility also highlights the importance of being clear about the two different purposes of assessment:

1. *Development*. The ongoing feedback and evaluation given to trainees during the course to clarify their skill strengths and weaknesses, to help them assess their learning needs and identify skills and competencies which they need to work on to reach the required standard.
2. *Qualification*. The final or summative assessments which qualify trainees as counsellors; their entry to the profession.

The course needs to clarify for the trainees the differences between the two modes, and also whether there are any assessments during the course which they must pass before proceeding to the next stage. There may also be ambiguity if the assessment of skills is ongoing throughout the course. Some courses keep records – or the students keep records – of each skills practice with comments and feedback and these are used for a final assessment. Again, it needs to be very clear to the trainees what is actually being assessed and when.

How does this role of 'gatekeeper' equate with the need for the trainer to model the core conditions?

RESPECT, ACCEPTANCE AND EVALUATION

Counselling, whatever the theory, is based on respect and acceptance of the client as a person, and we as trainers need to model this in our work with trainees. This creates difficulties when the trainer has to take on the role of assessor with authority and power to pass or fail. Dryden and Thorne (1991), writing on this issue, observe that:

> it is a formidable task to develop modes of evaluation which are at one and the same time sensitive to the trustworthiness of trainees, the insight and experience of trainers and the interests of future clients ... it demands a level of honesty and humility which is seldom achieved in any profession.

Being sensitive to the trustworthiness of the trainees may be shown by giving them the responsibility of self- and peer-assessment; it may also be shown, if the trainers are the sole assessors, by the *manner* in which the assessment is carried out. We return to this later.

What is the honesty and humility required by trainers? I think the honesty is about accepting our power and responsibility, being open with the trainees, talking with them how this power and responsibility can be shared with them, and how much still remains with us; how much trust we place in them, how they respond to this trust. The honesty is also about giving clear, specific, positive and negative feedback throughout the course to individuals, and checking that it is heard and understood. It is about owning our own expertise in stating what is good enough, what is excellent and what is not up to standard. You need to be clear about your 'standards' and how these match the standards of any fellow assessors. It could be useful to ask yourself:

- What exactly am I assessing?
- What is my idea of excellence in this?
- What is 'good enough for now'?
- What is 'not good enough but moving well towards it'?
- What is 'might develop with time'?
- What is 'necessary skills and qualities not developing'?
- How honest am I being with this trainee about my doubts?
- How does my judgement compare with my fellow trainers?
- How much have we compared our standards of evaluation?

Honesty is also about owning our ethical position, balancing caring for the trainee and caring for the future clients, and caring for the health of the counselling profession, the efficacy of which is at present being publicly questioned.

The humility, perhaps, is to know that we are not always right. We have blind spots and biases; some judgement must be subjective and our intuition can be questioned. We too are learners, struggling to do the best we can, hopefully acquainting ourselves with ideas and research which may make our assessments more reliable and more valid, and working towards more awareness of our possible blind spots.

MODES OF ASSESSMENT

It is likely that the more assessment is shared with trainer, trainee self-assessment and peers, the more equal will be the balance of power and responsibility. This may be particularly difficult if you are in an educational institution which has regulations regarding assessment for accredited courses; it may need sensitive, and tough, negotiation with the institution, if you want trainees to take all, or some, responsibility for their own learning and for assessment.

The balance of the power and responsibility for assessment is allocated differently in different courses, mainly depending on their philosophy, but also on possible institutional constraints. Below are some examples of a variety of modes of assessments.

Assessment in a person-centred course

The philosophy of a person-centred course is to empower clients by trusting them to take responsibility for their own development. So in training the trainees need to be trusted to take responsibility for their learning and for assessing their own development and competence.

One course which works in this way expects trainees to develop their own learning plans and their criteria for assessment which will qualify them as counsellors. The trainees use the trainers as a resource for learning and for help in identifying what they need to learn and work on; there is an emphasis on helping the trainees develop their own 'locus of evaluation', taking feedback from others but finding what is right for them. The trainees work with a small group of fellow trainees to help them set up the criteria which individually they need to meet to qualify. They also use this group to support, challenge and finally agree, or dispute, their own assessment of themselves. For assessment, each trainee produces a portfolio which demonstrates their learning and how they have reached the criteria set for themselves. The tutors take no part in the final assessment which rests on the individual trainees with their peers; the portfolios are seen by an external moderator who looks at overall standards and may negotiate with groups unable to agree on final assessments.

Assessment on an Integrative Course

Below is an example of a course which uses peer and self-assessment combined with tutor assessment, particularly for the assessment of the skills components, and uses tutor/supervisor assessment for client and written work. The tutor explained:

> Part of our assessment is joint assessment by self, peer and tutors. We state this in the student brochure and make it explicit on selection interviews so that it is part of the contract students accept if they come on the course.
>
> We set up the peer assessment structure at the end of the second term when students have had an opportunity to get to know each other. They have been in four allocated groups of five or six students for skills practice with feedback, for the first two terms. For next term they can choose their own groups; for 22 students last year we said two groups of six and two groups of five – that is their only limit.
>
> They will stay in the groups they choose until the end of the course and work in them weekly on skills and professional development. Those groups will be responsible for assessing each other on:
>
> (a) skills (including feedback skills);
> (b) on personal and professional development;
> (c) on contribution, skills and attitude in the large group.
>
> They will also read and comment on each other's case studies and audio-tapes which accompany the case studies. Work with clients is also assessed in the supervision groups which are different from their assessment groups. There is self-, peer- and supervisor-assessment in the supervision groups.
>
> We spend time at the end of the second term developing criteria with the students for each of these items – a difficult task, especially to agree what is the standard needed for a pass and what the criteria are for personal and professional development and in the large group. Last year our external moderator came in to the session, and this was useful for all of us.
>
> Students assess each other individually, writing clear feedback and comments and recommending pass, defer or borderline. Tutors do the same. Students also do a self-assessment, stating whether they think they are pass, defer or fail, commenting on their strengths and weaknesses and defining what learning they now want. If there is disagreement – and there usually is some – we negotiate and, if

necessary, call in the external moderator. The two core tutors are responsible for all the assessments and both assess all pieces of work. At the moment the tutors still assess the three pieces of written work and the final casestudies, though they have comments from students on the case studies. This is partly to satisfy our college requirements and maybe we will move eventually to negotiating for all work to be jointly assessed.

It is hard work; it brings up a lot of issues and some conflict within the group and with tutors. We as tutors need a lot of support from our supervision and from our external moderator. We now have a supportive new head of department who is interested in helping us develop and improve the way we manage this.

The courses illustrated above put all, or most, responsibility on the trainees for assessing whether they are competent to practise as a counsellor. This means considerable negotiation between staff and trainees both on criteria for standards to be reached and on methods to be used. Both also depend on an external moderator to help ensure the quality of the assessment and the standards. There seems to be a movement towards more self- and peer-assessment, but many courses still retain tutor assessment in whole or part. Below is an example of a course which has some peer and self assessment but relies mainly on tutors for the final assessment. The course tutor explained:

On my course skills training is intensive in the first year and evaluative feedback is given continuously by tutors and by peers; students are asked to do their own self-assessment. At the end of the first year, each student has to submit an audio-tape made with a colleague or with a 'real' client which demonstrates the three stages of skills from Egan's early Helping Model. It can be extracts from two sessions rather than one session covering all the skills. They also give in a record of the tutor- and peer-assessments they have received and their own assessment – what they feel competent at and what they still need to work at. The audio-tape is assessed by two tutors. If the tape is not satisfactory, they may have one more chance if their other assessments are a pass. If they do not pass this they cannot go on into the second year, as we believe they must have a good grasp of these basic skills at this stage.

All our students have done some basic training before entering the course, so we feel that if they are not at this stage now, they are not ready yet to complete the course. We make every effort to avoid failing anybody, and we do not have many students fail at this point, but, by experience, we have found when we let a doubtful student continue she has failed in the second year, and this is harder on the student and on the course.

At the end of the fifth term all students make a video-tape with a fellow student or with a client (we have some students on basic counselling courses who become clients for our trainees and they are sometimes willing to be videoed when they know how the tape will be used). The student gives in an analysis of what she did and why, what she likes about her style and what she wants to develop. The assessment procedure is that the video is seen with the student by a tutor who has not been her skills trainer, and who will question her during the showing against the following criteria:

1. Demonstrates a working alliance with the client; the work is a joint venture.
2. Shows evidence of a counselling relationship and some evidence of using the relationship in the session or in the analysis.
3. Demonstrates she can use the skills of the three-stage model, especially the 'action orientated' skills, and can integrate person-centred, TA or gestalt and give reasons why she has chosen the particular technique or skill.
4. Demonstrates that verbal and non-verbal behaviour are congruent, or she is aware of the incongruence.
5. Demonstrates the ability to begin and end the session and to pace and structure it.

The standard for a pass is 'sufficiently competent on all the criteria'. If there is doubt the video is seen by another tutor, or in some cases by the external examiner.

As part of the final assessment the student gives in a case study of a client with a 15-minute audio-tape extract from a session to demonstrate something the student feels she has done well.

When I look at your list of competencies I realize we do not directly assess some of them, though I think they are covered in supervision and could be included in the supervisor's report.

I think we are satisfied with our assessment procedures for skills but maybe the final assessment should be on skills used in their client work. We have reasonable access to video and like to use that to see the student working and this is not usually possible with real clients. The assessment places quite a burden on individual tutors but we think it is important to allocate time to this.

In this example there is considerable focus on assessing specific skills and how they are used with a client.

The next example is from a psycho-dynamic course which has a wider form of assessment. The tutor said:

We have no formal assessment of skills but continuous feedback and evaluation is done by tutors and peers during the skills groups which finish at the end of the first year. From the feedback, each student writes up a self-evaluation of his skills which is discussed in an end of year tutorial, together with his progress in the course. For the final assessment, skills with clients are assessed by a supervisor's report and by a case study with a verbatim account of one session with analysis. This is given in during the last term. The case study and verbatim needs to demonstrate that the students are working beyond the basic skills, have a sound therapeutic relationship with the client and are aware of their own process in the interaction. Two assessors read the case study and verbatim and the supervisor's report; they then have a tutorial with the student to explore his work in more depth and make the final assessment. We place as much emphasis on self-awareness skills as on communication skills in our assessment.

Supervision is in groups of four with one supervisor; verbatim records of sessions and role-play are both used in the groups so the supervisor will have some good knowledge of the students' skills. We put a lot of emphasis on the student being able to integrate his skills with his theory learning and know why he is using them at that point in a session, also his ability to explore unconscious processes within the session.

This course relies much more on supervision, both for learning skills and for assessment and does not require audio or video, but uses verbatim recording to check which skills are being used with clients.

This gives you some idea of the range of possibilities for assessment; Dryden and Thorne (1991) provide examples of complete peer assessment in Chapter 4 and of self-assessment in Chapters 3 and 5. Chapter 5 also gives examples of the range of modes of assessment which exist in different diploma courses.

These are some of the structures and some of the criteria used across the field. Let's move on to exploring some other issues on assessment.

IS ASSESSMENT POSSIBLE BY 'PERFORMANCE' CRITERIA?

Is counselling an art or a science? This is one of the big issues of discussion – and disagreement. If it is an art, can a counsellor be assessed by setting up performance criteria? Can the 'qualities' and 'intention' of the counsellor be measured in this way, or only the observable skills?

Dryden and Feltham (1994), addressed the assessment of skills training:

With increasing attention being given to nationally and interprofessionally validated skills, we believe that identification and measurement of such competencies will become an unavoidable aspect of the counsellor trainer's responsibilities. (p. 61)

Russell (1993) replying to comments about 'efforts to monitor qualities that many feel to be elusive and unquantifiable' has expressed the opinion that: 'it is no longer plausible to say that the measurement of competent practice is elusive and unquantifiable ... if counselling is teachable, it is identifiable and its competent use observable. If it is not, then we must query the validity of counselling courses'. We have accepted that skills are teachable and observable, therefore it is possible to assess whether this student can perform these skills – we can even mark them off on a list. But, we have also accepted that performance of the skills must be linked with 'intention' – the ability of the student to select from a repertoire of skills the appropriate ones to further the work with the client at that moment. This may be a composite of skills: the ability to discriminate what is going on in the client, what is going on in himself, what theory will help to produce the desired outcome, what pace or intensity is required – the final result is much more an artistic creation than a set of skills. How can we assess this? We cannot normally assess the outcome by asking the client, and that might not be a reliable assessment. In the US counsellors are usually trained attached to a counselling agency where free or low-cost on-going clients agree to be videoed and are sometimes asked to comment on the counsellor; supervision with the video provides ongoing feedback and assessment for the student. This is unknown or rare in this country, and, usually we can only have access to the work with the client second-hand, by hearing an audio-tape which the trainee may have reflected on and analyzed, by reading the trainee's case and process recording, by his or her supervision presentation and reflection, perhaps by ongoing records of skill development with fellow students. Some possibilities for methods of assessment are set out in Table 7.1. You may like to consider which assessments would give a valid picture of whether the trainee is skilled and competent enough to become a qualified counsellor.

Table 7.1 *Possible methods of skills assessment.* All of these methods can be trainer-, peer- or self-assessment, or different combinations of these

---

First-hand

1. The student does a 'live' session with a colleague, either using his or her own material or role-playing a client. The assessors watch and viva with the student afterwards.

2. Similar session, but on video, watched through a one-way screen. Viva with the student afterwards.

3. On-going assessment throughout the course of specific skills, within the skills group; trainees counselling each other.

Second-hand
3. Similar session made on video, without one-way screen and replayed straight-away to assessors with viva.
4. Similar session made on video but at any time prior to assessment. The student may make several videos and choose one to bring. All or part played back to assessors during viva.
5. Audio-tape of session with colleague, made for assessment and replayed straight away during viva.
6. Audio-tape of session with colleague, pre-recorded, analyzed and verbatim written recording made; given to assessors to assess with or without the student present for viva.
7. Audio-tape of session with real client pre-recorded as above.
8. Audio-tape of first session with a client showing introducing self and counselling and making a contract.
9. Audio-tape of an IPR session (see Appendix 1) showing 'process' awareness.
10. Audio-tape with client or student role-play demonstrating 'theory'-based techniques, e.g. using visualization, using 'force field analysis', 'disputing' for Rational Emotive Therapy (RET).

Third-hand
11. Verbatim written recording of session with client, with analysis, process recording, self-evaluation given to assessors, with or without tutorial.
12. Verbatim recording of 8. 9. or 10. above.
13. Case notes, case studies, giving examples of skills used, with or without tutorial.
14. Records of ongoing evaluation and feedback from skills groups with or without self-evaluation, with or without tutorial.
15. Supervisors'/peers' reports of skills ability of supervisee as demonstrated in the supervision group.
16. Trainers'/peers' reports of skills ability in experiential sessions relating to theory or professional development.
17. Facilitators'/peers' reports of skills ability in personal development group or community group.
18. Records of self-awareness or self-management development extracted from personal learning journal.
19. Written records of work done in professional development group, e.g. work on referral.
20. Written examinations or tests on skills knowledge and use.
21. Written papers demonstrating knowledge of a range of skills and when and when not to use them – examples from use with different clients.

Many of these items could be included in a portfolio presented for assessment to peers or trainers.
There is an example of an assessment form for assessing a cognitive therapist in Dryden and Feltham (1994) Appendix 4, using a scale of 0 – 6.

WHAT IS A VALID ASSESSMENT?

Does the assessment measure what it sets out to measure? Or are we using forms of assessment which are convenient, traditional or possible within the constraints of the training agency? Are we really assessing whether this student is 'fit to practise' as a counsellor? Connor (1994) states:

> Predictive validity is an important aspect of assessment and trainers should try to develop those assessment procedures which will provide evidence of what the trainee can, predictably, do in the real counselling situation. Counsellor trainers need to look carefully at their existing assessment processes and procedures ... does the sum total of assessment processes actually assess counsellor competence? Or does it assess idiosyncratic elements of training which it has been thought would be easy to assess? (p. 161)

She cites research by Lambert (1989):

> that the *skilfulness* of the counsellor [my italics] may be an essential element leading to successful outcome in the client, despite technique, theoretical position or client predisposition towards counselling ... they recommend that assessment procedures need to focus upon individual attributes and skills so that it is possible to identify those trainees who would have a negative effect on client outcome. (p. 161)

From this it seems that lack of skills may be the most likely prediction of poor counselling outcomes. Does this then indicate that the assessment of skills is central to designing valid assessment procedures, more important than the counsellor's understanding of theory or ability with techniques? And how can we assess whether the skills are really built into the trainee's repertoire? That he or she is 'unconsciously competent' and can maintain these skills, not just 'consciously competent' for the purposes of assessment.

Also, as we have said above, it is comparatively easy to assess discrete skills demonstrated in real or role-played course sessions, and skill development can also be measured by written tests (Carkhuff, 1969a), but is this a valid assessment of how skilled the trainee is with real clients? Also, do all the competencies listed in Table 1.1 need to be assessed, and if so how could this be done? Is a counsellor not 'fit' unless he or she can do them all?

There is also the question of how skills assessment fits in with the whole assessment – what weighting should it have? Can it be separated? For example, if methods of assessing progress in skills include case studies, case notes, personal learning journals and supervision, are there clear criteria or can it only be a more general subjective impression assessment?

These are issues which the advent of NVQs is bringing to the surface, which trainers will be struggling with and debating, whatever the eventual outcome of the acceptance or not of NVQs as qualifications.

WHAT IS A RELIABLE ASSESSMENT?

A reliable assessment is one that would be repeatable, producing the same results with different assessors. If the assessment is by a combination of self-assessment by the trainee, peer and trainers, all working to the same clear criteria, within a climate of openness and commitment to the responsibility, it is likely to be more reliable. If the assessment is by one trainer it may not be so reliable – bias or skewed judgement is possible.

Courses which rely on trainer assessment usually ensure that all work is assessed independently by two trainers, or one trainer and an outside assessor. This can be very time-consuming for video or audio-tapes, especially if the tape is seen or heard with the trainee and commented upon. Some courses compromise on this by one trainer assessing, with or without a viva with the trainee, and only calling in another opinion if it is not a clear pass. Another issue is whether skills trainers should assess their own trainees, or should it be another staff member, and how might this affect the trust between staff and trainees?

Trainers, however hard they work to remain objective, may become biased for or against a trainee. Paradoxically, the more the trainee is known as a person, the more difficult it may be for the trainer to be objective in assessments. Projection, identification, transference and counter-transference could all be hazards, however authentic we work to be, so lone assessment may not be fair or reliable. This has implications for staffing and for costing.

I find in many courses, especially those staffed by part-time staff, that assessment is often done as unpaid overtime and I think this denigrates the importance of the gatekeeper role. Course design needs to build assessment firmly into the timetable and structure, recognizing and accepting the judgement it implies, and the amount of time required for negotiation when self- and peer-assessment is involved.

Manner of setting up assessment

Another issue to consider which may affect reliability is the manner in which the assessment is set up.

I mentioned this early in the chapter. Assessment is stressful for most individuals; many adults have had unpleasant earlier experiences. Some courses say counselling is a stressful occupation, and a certain amount of stress around assessment shows how well the trainee can manage. Other courses make assessment procedures as gentle as possible, and trainers use all their facilitation skills to help trainees give their best on assessment. More sensitive trainees – often good counsellor material – may not produce their best, especially in live situations on video. What do you believe? What structures do you set up which may cause or alleviate stress? What allowances do you make? Do you encourage trainees to assess your competency as a trainer and what does that bring up for you?

To grade or not to grade

A final thought on the issue of reliability is the question of grading; another delicate issue. Grades can promote competitiveness, arouse the perfectionists, can be another source of unreliability, create more work for the assessors, emphasize the judgement element, and can extend students towards excellence, give merit where merit is due and reward hard work. Your institution may demand grades or clear feedback may make them unnecessary.

If you are going to grade the following are possibilities:

- Percentage marks with stated percentage for a pass.
- Graded 1–5; 3 is a pass, 4 borderline and 5 fail.
- Pass, border-line, defer, fail.
- Pass or fail.
- Remarks, no pass or fail.

Sometimes when I ask why a course is graded by percentages or A–F, the answer is, because that is how it has always been, the students like it, and the staff have never considered what would happen if they just gave pass/defer/fail. Or, with another course which had no grades, only remarks – what is a fail? As long as students submitted the required tape, paper, journal, case study, they passed. The assessment was whether the training staff felt intuitively the student was OK as a counsellor. And maybe that is as good assessment as any! Where are you on this issue – or where are you allowed to be?

Appendix 2 contains examples of competency assessment forms used on one course and there is a form for peer-assessment of basic counselling skills.

CHAPTER QUESTIONS

The following questions may help you clarify where you stand:

1. How clear are the assessment procedures for new trainees?
2. Is there on-going assessment of skills throughout the course? Half-way assessments? Final assessments?
3. Who is assessing? Staff, peers, trainees themselves? If a combination what weight will each carry and how is this negotiated?
4. What exactly is being assessed under the skills heading?
5. Are the criteria clear for each assessment?
6. What is the role of the external assessor (if any)?
7. Are we satisfied as a staff team that the assessments are as reliable and valid as we can make them at this time?

EIGHT

Who are you as a skills trainer?

In this last chapter I want to explore what makes a good skills trainer. What are the personal qualities, attitudes and beliefs, skills, competencies, and background which ensure the sort of trainer who can empower, engage and enskill trainees? Finally, I will look at ways to become a skills trainer and to continue professional development.

ROLES AND ARCHETYPES

Figure 8.1 shows the multitude of roles in which you may engage as skills trainer. Some are unavoidable, some may be only fleeting engagements, some you will enjoy, and some you may find do not suit you as a person. How you play each of these roles will depend on how you have developed as a person, what influences have shaped you and, partly, on what is your underlying temperament e.g. whether you are an extrovert or an introvert, a natural leader or natural follower.

Figure 8.1 also shows some archetypes, some identified by Proctor (in Dryden and Thorne, 1991, Chapter 4), as possibly being part of the trainer personality. Another way of looking at how you play the roles may be by exploring which archetypes fit for you, which you might develop or which perhaps you have outgrown. Exploring these may open new worlds, and give new insights into the way of being as trainer.

I will explore the skills and competencies for the roles and then take a brief look at the archetypes.

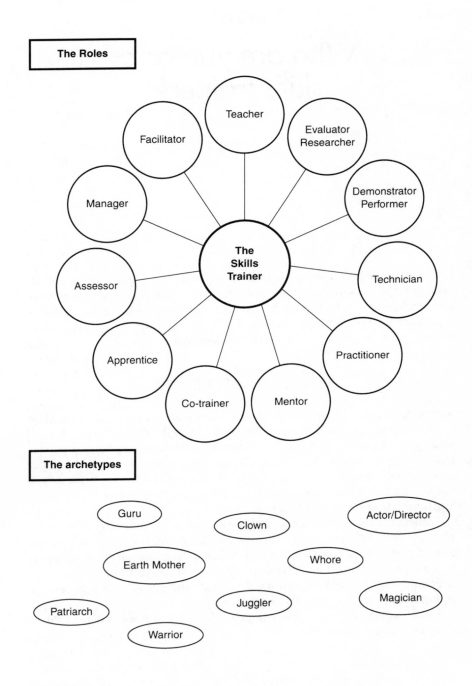

Figure 8.1

Roles

The skills and competencies you need for many of these roles have been mentioned in the preceding chapters, and I will add some extra thoughts here.

As *model/demonstrator/performer* you need to be competent at all the skills you will be helping the trainees to learn, you need to be confident with your competence – and consciously competent. I mentioned earlier that when the trainer becomes unconsciously competent it is often hard to dissect the skill and make it accessible to trainees. Building and maintaining these skills, and acquiring new ones, requires commitment to on-going learning – and trainees are often the greatest teachers! If you are naturally shy and do not want to impose your ideas on others (a counsellor quality), you may find performing hard and so avoid the role. However, you will be asking trainees to perform and role-play in front of you and they appreciate a trainer who is willing to take the same risks. If you have avoided this role and have justified it, perhaps as not wanting to produce 'clones', you might want to consider what it would cost you to change and what you, and the trainees, might gain from you risking a new role. If you decide to try it out, you will need to consider how you might practise to build up your confidence.

As *manager* you need to be competent at setting up structures, giving orders and instructions, negotiating for space and equipment (often includes moving the furniture), a good mathematician (able to divide 19 trainees into groups of twos, threes or fours!), timing and pacing a session, seeing the coffee urn is filled, nurturing and directing video technicians, and negotiating sharing all these tasks, and others, with trainees and other staff. This role requires taking and using authority without being 'bossy', using leadership skills, knowing when to be assertive and when to give ground, and the ability to delegate and to get others to cooperate with you. It requires all the communication and interpersonal skills, including clear purpose and preference stating. Skills training usually requires some familiarity with video and audio equipment, or the ability to manage technicians to cooperate with you and the trainees.

As *facilitator* you will need especially the communication and interpersonal skills and especially all the skills mentioned in Chapter 6 on working in a group. The facilitator's role is to enable the group to work on the task, whatever that is, and the first skill is to help the group be clear what is the task. You will need to be able to switch from manager/teacher/leader roles to a more receptive and listening role of helping trainees express themselves, of clarifying, making space for reticent trainees to come in, holding boundaries of safety and time. This is the important role when the whole course is negotiating the sharing of structuring, teaching, and assessing. It is a difficult role to play when you are also part of the group with equal decision making power to the trainees – if this is the agreement. What needs to be very clear in this type of negotiation is exactly how much power is shared; you as facilitator will be responsible for clarifying this. Because you take different roles in different groups, you are also responsible for clarifying your exact role as facilitator in this group, and how much power and authority you have, and how you will use it.

As *teacher* you will need skills of designing and preparing skills learning sessions, of producing handouts and overhead-projection transparencies to back up the learning, of writing legibly on flip-charts or wall boards and of finding, creating and using resources for demonstrating skills.

You will also need the skill of describing skills clearly, how and when to use them, how they can be integrated into work with clients and when not to use them. You will need a repertoire of activities for practising skills, abilities to devise role-plays for specific skills, and to be able to give very clear instructions when setting up activities. Trainees are often very anxious when starting exercises or activities, and you need to be especially clear in explaining what they are expected to do, for how long, who will time if necessary, etc. If you do not like telling people to do things this will be hard for you, if you are naturally bossy be careful to moderate it! Giving clear instructions for activities needs practice; if you are new to this find ways of trying it out on somebody and getting feedback. I find when training new trainers, especially if they come from a counsellor background, becoming competent and confident at giving clear instructions to a group of trainees, without oppressing them, is one of the hardest skills to master – and one of the skills trainees consider important. I think it is linked with attitudes to being an authority which we will consider later.

You will also need the skill of giving feedback which the trainee can hear and use, and managing your time to give attention to each trainee. It may also be important to find ways of keeping records of trainee progress and of any ongoing assessments which will be used for final qualification.

As *co-trainer* you need all your communication and interpersonal skills, especially the second-stage ones of self-disclosure and immediacy, so that you build an open and authentic relationship which includes challenge and support.

Deciding how you will share the roles will be important. If you complement each other in your abilities or preferences, e.g. one good at managing, one good at facilitating, this may be easy. If you are similar in style and preferences you will have to negotiate and learn how to accommodate each other.

You will need to commit time to planning together and to reflecting on your work afterwards. With one of my co-trainers, we agree at the beginning of each course what specific learning we each want as a trainer from this experience, and we spend time at the end helping each other explore our learning. This has been an important part of my ongoing professional development. Joint supervision is often very helpful in having a third person to help reflection and planning ahead, and sometimes to help disentangle feelings of competition or inferiority.

I said earlier that co-training can be a very rich experience, but it can also be a difficult one while the working alliance is building. You will both be exposed to transference and projections from the trainees, and from each other probably, at times. When difficulties arise some trainees may revert to skills they learnt as children to split or manipulate parents, and this provides wonderful material for 'games'. I have sometimes found the best way of cutting into the 'games' is to 'goldfish-bowl' with my co-trainer, talking with each other as if the trainees are not there, and after some discussion providing two extra chairs for any of the group to join in the discussion in turn. This can promote more authenticity in the group – and has its risks!

I recommend co-training strongly for trainer professional development, for entry to training, for its creative possibilities in finding new ways of training, and for the benefit of trainees.

As *trainer of an apprentice-trainer* you will be inducting a new trainer into the profession with all that that implies. It needs the skills of a co-trainer as above, but also needs skills of sharing work, giving enough practice without deskilling the new trainer or the trainees, making time for reflection and encouragement and giving honest and caring feedback.

To empower the new trainer so that you are each clear on your responsibilities, may need a clear contract between you on how you will work and, it may be necessary to clarify what specific learning he or she needs – and what you might learn in return. The learning outside the session might include recommending resources and reading, and perhaps making available some of your experience and learning.

As *apprentice-trainee* you need to be a highly motivated learner, a good observer, reflector and questioner, willing to risk yourself in a new role, and flexible to fit in with your mentor, but assertive enough to ask for what you want. You need to be confident in being competent enough in all the skills you will be required to help the trainees learn. You will need to be thinking back to how you learnt counsellor skills, comparing your mentor's way of working and trying what is right for you – and for the trainees.

Besides being able to reflect on your work with your trainer mentor, you will need to use supervision to enhance your learning, and increase your knowledge by appropriate reading and any training available. Your skills will be in finding creative ways to pass on your experience and learning to the trainees, and in relating to the group from this particular role.

As *assessor* your integrity is vital. You need to be clear where you stand on the moral principles referred to by Bond (1993, p. 33):

1. *Beneficence*: What will achieve the greatest good?
2. *Non-maleficence*: What will cause least harm?

3. *Justice*: What will be fairest?
4. *Respect for autonomy*: What maximizes the opportunities for everyone involved to implement their own choices?

In making decisions on structures, criteria and levels of acceptable competence it is useful to consider these principles and how to balance the rights and needs of the trainee, the clients, the training course, and the profession. No easy task!

One important skill is knowing the level of competence you expect from the trainees, clarifying this for them, devising, negotiating, agreeing criteria for skill assessment, and being able to assess as objectively as possible. You will also need to set up assessment procedures, negotiate how peer- and self-assessment will be done, if this is course policy, and keep appropriate records.

Assessing audio- or video-recordings of client work and the analysis by the trainee, requires concentration – and good recording equipment. It is always partly subjective, however clearly the criteria are defined. You need to clarify for yourself what you believe is helpful to the client. What does your intuition tell you is going on between them? Are you looking for positive helping? Will you pass this, providing there are no negative indications from this trainee? What is your bottom line? It is the borderline trainees that require careful judgement and ethical consideration.

As one of a team of trainers you may need to decide with others if this trainee will qualify. How clear and confident can you be on your judgements? How flexible? If you fail this trainee and there is an appeal are you clear on the criteria you have used?

As *counsellor practitioner* your skill will be in reflecting on your counselling, taking your learning from that to help the trainees integrate the micro-skills they learn and practise into responding with skill and understanding to their clients. You need to find ways of using examples from your work without divulging confidentiality. To use your counselling to enhance your training skills and to use your learning as a trainer to enhance your counselling. It is also a skill to manage your time so that you still have time to work as a counsellor, even though the training may make heavy demands on you. Working with clients helps the skills trainer keep the importance of integrating skills in the forefront, and of recognizing that the outcome of skills training is for the client to get the best possible service from the counsellor.

As *technician* skill and practice in using video or audio equipment is well worth acquiring, however ignorant and incapable you believe you are. It is also useful to pass these skills on to trainees. For the non-technically minded, it may be an opportunity to experience being consciously incompetent!

As *evaluator/researcher* you need skills to devise ways of finding out if the methods you use to train in skills really do produce the outcomes you hope for. To evaluate your training you need to obtain verbal or written feedback from trainees, perhaps on specific training methods, and on you as teacher, manager, facilitator etc. You could also get help on evaluating the course from other staff, perhaps from trainers from another course, and from the external moderator.

Research can be an important part of your professional development as a skills trainer, and could make a contribution to the profession, especially at this time of questioning standards of counselling and the setting up of NVQs for counsellors. There has been very little research on whether the trainee who demonstrates good micro-skills in practice on the course is better than 'poorer performers' in integrating these into work with clients.

Much of the research which has been done on micro-skills has been on the training in 'counselling skills'. Is the time allocated to micro-skills in diploma courses the best way of training counsellors, as opposed to training other professionals who want to learn counselling skills? Doing small research projects as a trainer also provides a good model for the trainee counsellor.

Archetypes: How do the archetypes influence how you play the roles?

- '*Guru*' or '*wise woman*'. Do you aspire to this – or are you allocated it by the trainees, by other trainers? Does your experience, age or wisdom fit you for this way of being? Can you use it to empower others, or does it always disempower? What do you feel about this archetype?

- '*Clown*'. Are you an entertainer? Do you provide fun and jokes? Are you able to go with the sadness and absurdity of life and stimulate thinking by using riddles and metaphors in your teaching? Have you a clown you keep hidden as not appropriate for training? Might it be useful at times, or might it disrupt the task?

- '*Earth mother*'. Are you a natural nurturer, a safe harbour when needed in storms, a provider of good handouts to feed the hungry? Is there more support than challenge in the way you play your trainer roles? Or could you develop this archetype if needed?

- '*Actor/director*'. Are you a natural performer, acting out each role with energy, or a director allocating the roles and task to others, wanting to produce a 'good performance' and develop your cast? How does this help or hinder you as a trainer?

- '*Patriarch*'. Do you naturally enjoy power and creating order? Are you a natural leader able to wield power without being oppressive? Can you use this in some roles and cast it aside in others? Can you exercise power elegantly and appropriately?

- '*Whore*'. Do you use seduction to encourage trainees to take risks? Do you change your affections easily as you move from one group of trainees to the next? Do you use your 'attractiveness' (social influence) to empower or disempower?
- '*Warrior*'. Do you search and fight for 'truth', carry a banner for the counselling profession, take clear ethical standpoints? Do you enjoy conflict and challenge – and promote them? Can you use anger well and model this for others? Can you let the Warrior rest at times? Can you find one when needed, or have you never developed this archetype and do not wish to?
- '*Magician*' who produces the rabbit from the hat. The training is so brilliantly and smoothly conducted the trainees are entranced. But are they empowered?
- '*Juggler*'. Are you adept at doing and thinking several things at once, balancing work, relationships and time for self? Do you like the limelight? Can you keep 12 trainees in your head at once? Can you teach, perform, facilitate and manage, all in one session? Can you use right and left brain at the same time? (Practising juggling is supposed to develop the right side of the brain.) Might this archetype be useful to you – or encourage you to take on too much? (I have to send my Juggler away for regular holidays!)

These are some archetypes, you may think of more. Speedy (unpublished dissertation, Bristol University, 1993) did some research with 13 women trainers of counselling and counselling skills, on their concepts of power. She used the archetypes of 'heroine', 'healer', 'harlot' and 'hag' which may give you further ideas.

QUALITIES OF THE 'IDEAL' TRAINER

As a trainer, who are you surrounded by all these roles and archetypes? Does this exploration help you to think about what qualities, abilities, competencies you have and what you might like, or need to develop? To further this exploration it may be useful to know what trainees want from a skills trainer. These are some of the comments I had from several courses:

Ability to help the group feel safe. Set up and keep a good structure. Liveliness. The ability to be open enough to be seen as a genuine person. To let the trainees be heard. To accept and respect trainees as individuals. To create fun. Expertness, but not too much. To hold structure and be 'bossy' when needed, but not authoritarian. To bring energy to the group. To demonstrate and take part in role-play. Good pace to prevent boredom, space for talking out issues but not too much. To be warm and friendly but not 'one of the boys'. To inspire into risks and experiential work. To be enthusiastic, and have common sense. To bring examples from own experience. To give clear instructions and helpful feedback. To enjoy the work. And finally give good handouts.

In contrast, the following comments are from trainees on what they do *not* want from trainers:

The trainer to justify when challenged. To be made to feel stupid if they questioned anything. To be put 'in the wrong'. Not to know what was expected for assessment, to have the 'goal-posts' moved. To be left to practise without any feedback from the trainer. Lack of structure and timing. A timid trainer. More counsellor than trainer. A therapy group instead of a training session. A monotonous voice. Inability to control the group, or protect members when necessary.

These comments may give some food for thought on how to become this paragon, which leads me on to the final section:

BECOMING A SKILLS TRAINER: HOW DO YOU GET IN AND WHAT DO YOU NEED?

I meet many trainers in the course of my work and often ask them how they came into the role; there is no direct route as there is, for instance, into school teaching or nurse training. In 1988, the BAC set up a working party to explore training for trainers and as a result published two information sheets, suggesting what content courses for trainers should contain: 'A. Courses for counsellors with no substantial adult education experience/expertise, wishing to run counselling training' and 'C. Master Degree courses for counsellor trainers' (both obtainable from the BAC).

The Working Party found at that time no ongoing course for trainers, but only a few short courses, often run as summer workshops. There is now at least one Master Course which focuses on training and supervision of counsellors, entry normally requiring a diploma in counselling. This lack of training was identified then, and the need has become greater since with the rise in the number of Diploma Courses requiring skilled, experienced trainers.

In the early days of counsellor training, courses were often staffed by psychologists (clinical and educational), social workers, careers guidance staff, marriage guidance counsellors, health visitors, nurse tutors, teacher trainers, psychotherapists, chaplains and other clergy. There is still a wide range of professions contributing to counsellor training, but most have now done some training in counselling if they come from education, and if they come from counselling, may have done some training in adult education.

Many enter by working on short counselling skills training courses and this can be good experience to become a skills trainer on a counsellor course. However, it would seem very important that the trainer has at least the equal to the qualification he is training for, i.e. at least a diploma in counselling.

Anybody wanting to move into a training role needs to look carefully at the counsellor diploma courses offered. Some diploma courses are recognized by the BAC and these should provide good training. There is a BAC booklet available, *The Recognition of Training Courses*, which details what is required for a recognized course, and this could be a useful guide in exploring possible courses. Many colleges offer part-time courses in adult education. These can be very helpful in developing the skills and abilities for all the roles mentioned above, especially for working on courses which are partly or wholly student-managed.

Working over an extended period of two or three years with trainees who are in the process of accelerated change and development, can be emotionally and mentally challenging. Trainers need to have already completed some of this growth themselves, and although there is always more to do, the trainer needs some emotional stability and toughness to be able to work with, and contain a group of trainees. A prospective trainer, who is not already in counselling, could well start some counselling to explore motivation and 'holding capacity', attitudes towards being in authority, and to being visible and vulnerable in a group; this could also be a useful experience of the client role.

It is important to recognize that the role of trainer is very different from the role of counsellor and requires extra skills, besides all the skills knowledge, and attitudes of a counsellor. When you have the right qualifications the finest way of learning is to apprentice yourself to a good trainer – or to several good trainers, might be even better.

ON-GOING PROFESSIONAL DEVELOPMENT

If you are already in the role, how do you develop as a skills trainer? A masters course is one possibility or the few short courses available. It is noticeable that since the BAC set up a recognition procedure for supervisors, courses for supervisors are blossoming in many parts of the country. In 1989 I was part of a working group to set up a procedure for the recognition of trainers, and this was piloted, but was found too expensive to maintain and has been shelved. However, there is a BAC working group looking at a simpler procedure and maybe when this comes to fruition, courses for trainers will be generated. I hope so.

In the meantime, networking with other trainers, conferences, short courses, reading, writing, producing videos which demonstrate skills, setting up working groups to develop resources or explore assessment of skills – all these widen experience and could help us to help trainees become caring, competent counsellors who can help clients live more zestfully and effectively.

Writing this book has caused me to read, think and question, and so has been an important professional development for me – I hope it may also contribute to your development. I will welcome any feedback.

APPENDIX 1

Structures and techniques for teaching and practising skills

This appendix gives some structures and techniques I and other trainers have found useful in helping students learn and practise skills. I have gone into their use in some detail and you may find some helpful ideas, even if you have met them before.

STRUCTURE FOR PRACTICE WITH FEEDBACK

The first is known as the Gilmore group and is one of the best structures I have found for helping students learn and practise skills. It comes from *The Counsellor in Training* (Gilmore, 1973), an old book now – and American, which most were then – but still very useful. There is a practicum of 12 three-hour sessions described in the book, much of which I have used and adapted in various ways throughout my training work, but the part which I have passed on to many trainers is the small group structure for actual counselling practice.

The structure consists ideally of a group of six with a trainer. I have used up to eight when I have had three hours weekly, but it is not ideal.

It is probably better to divide them into two groups and move between them, as Brian in his example divided his group of eleven. Pauline, who uses this structure some of the time with 24 students, has four groups and trainee tutors taking two of them.

The structure for working in the group is set out in Table A1.1.

The contract for the group

1. Confidentiality within the group. The tutor may discuss the process of the group and progress of students with other staff or supervisor, but not the content of the counselling sessions.

2. Students will in turn be clients for each other for short sessions (10–20 minutes, depending on the skills to be practised), and will be responsible for bringing their own material. (Gilmore in her book sets homework for students to work on and bring issues arising from that to work on as a client. One example on next page.)
3. Students will take it in turns to counsel, practising the skills.
4. The observers will give positive and negative feedback, when possible as a sandwich (positive – negative – positive), and keep to the structure.
5. All students and the tutor will give written feedback to each other on the last session of the term:
   (a) on the counselling skills observed;
   (b) on the feedback skills they have observed;
   (c) on their perception of the development of empathy, respect and genuineness in each other, using a scale of 1–5 and comments.
6. Students will write up a self-assessment on these three areas and share this with the group.

The written feedback is given out at the beginning of the last session and the students and tutor meet in pairs with everybody in the group and talk about any issues arising from the written feedback. This means ongoing notes need to be kept by students on their own and on each other's progress.

Table A1.1 *Structure for the Gilmore group*

---

1. Counsellor and client arrange themselves so that they are out of eye contact with the group, but can be heard and seen. Time is agreed and the counsellor can keep time or ask for a timekeeper.

2. At the end of the session everybody, including the client and counsellor and tutor, has three or four minutes to write down feedback.

3. The observers then give their feedback in turn with the tutor last, reading what they have written even if it repeats others' observations.

4. The client gives feedback.

5. The counsellor summarizes all the feedback without commenting. The observers and client remind the counsellor if any is forgotten.

6. The counsellor gives her own thoughts on the session.

7. A brief space for any issues, not going back to 'the case', but particularly any learning which has come up for individuals, and some brief time for writing if needed.

Advantages of this structure

- Everybody is working all the time – it is hard work being an observer, trying to remember specific things.
- It emphasizes the importance of feedback and provides a norm for everybody to give positive and negative feedback to each other.
- The structure can be adapted to any skills work, e.g. using video instead of live counselling.
- Students can work on their own for part of the time without the tutor.
- It can provide a structure in student-managed courses for the students to set up their own skills work and use the trainers as a resource.

The tutor's role is to maintain the structure, to join in as counsellor or client when appropriate, and to model skills and give feedback. To draw out any learning issues not brought in by the group and to teach skills if necessary. As the group progresses, the tutor may give more time for exploring when to use different skills and how they relate to the theory being taught, also to make time for, and help, the group to examine and be aware of the 'process' of the group as the group develops.

Some people see it as a rigid structure, especially if they are not happy with a task group and want to spend more time on 'process', but most appreciate it as a good learning structure for skills practice. It has an emphasis on the skills of feedback, and it gives opportunities for the clients to explore something real and relevant for them within clear boundaries.

The main body of the Gilmore book contains some useful work on exploring how we can develop and build the core qualities in ourselves – understanding (empathy), acceptance (respect/unconditional positive regard) and sincerity (congruence, genuineness) – and the homework is based on reading and activities related to these. You will need to obtain the book to get all the details, but one exercise I have found useful for developing 'acceptance' is to ask the students to plan and undertake a 'new experience'. Something which will extend their experience of the unfamiliar, something they are prejudiced about, or something they fear. They bring back to the group not an anecdote of the experience, but the feelings aroused in them and any change of perceptions of themselves or others. Individuals seem to learn and internalize a lot from this exercise and new experiences have ranged from 'going to a bingo session' where a prejudiced young man saw the warm interaction and fun it brought to many peoples lives, especially the elderly, to a woman prejudiced against the Christian church spending a day with a vicar in the East End of London doing the rounds of his parish, to experiencing what it was like being in a wheelchair for a day. This exercise encourages creativity and a recognition of how we need to move into other worlds if we are to be understanding and accepting of a wider range of people.

Pauline, who has used this structure over a number of years, said:

I keep a tight structure at the beginning, especially for practising the basic counselling skills. The students have done quite a bit of work in the large group watching demonstrations, trying some skills in pairs, learning feedback skills and getting to know each other in the large group.

When I move into small groups I spend the first session with my group going over the structure and the contract with them, doing some fun exercises to get to know each a bit more, going over feedback skills and letting them give feedback on a taped session which has a mixture of good and bad skills and then asking for a volunteer to counsel me so that I demonstrate the client role. The volunteer will not get feedback but we spend time discussing the client role. We then arrange who will counsel whom over the next two sessions, taking three counsellors each week, so by week three all will have been counsellor and client. I will not join in as counsellor until they have all had a go.

Our skills sessions are one and a half hours, so on the next sessions we do three rounds taking about 25 minutes for each round and leaving 15 minutes at the end to explore the 'process' of the group. For the next six weeks we do two rounds each session and have longer for issues and group process. We use the last week for exchanging written feedback and meeting briefly in pairs to discuss it. That takes about 50 minutes and we then come back to the group and each shares their self-assessment with the group and identifies what they want to work on next.

We had great difficulties with peer- and self-assessment before we used this structure, but it now becomes a norm from the beginning of the course.

TECHNIQUES FOR DEVELOPING SELF-AWARENESS WITHIN THE COUNSELLING SESSION

One of the most difficult skills for students to learn seems to be the ability to use their inner awareness in interaction with the client and communicate this appropriately to the client. It is more important in some counselling theories than others, but is a skill all counsellors need so that they can develop a working alliance that is a genuine partnership with the client. Making the process of counselling as open and unmystical as possible shares the responsibility of the work with the client, promotes the autonomy of the client and often helps when the session seems to be stuck. How this is done and in what detail obviously depends on the state of the client and the situation. It often feels risky and against the norms of usual interaction, so needs plenty of practice for both the awareness and the communication skills.

Interpersonal Process Recall

I have found this to be one of the best techniques for training in these skills. It is a training technique which can help students develop:

- internal awareness – what is happening inside them in interactions;
- awareness of what is happening between them and a client in the relationship;
- skills to express this awareness appropriately to the client;
- an internal supervisor;
- a monitoring process to help them use supervision;
- an awareness of when they feel real and genuine in a situation and when they feel false, and the difficulties of expressing this.

Interpersonal Process Recall (IPR) is a training method developed by Norman Kagan (Kagan, 1975) in the 1970s, not specifically for counselling but for interpersonal work in the helping professions. It is fairly widely used in training but not always used in all its possibilities, so I set out here methods I have adapted and used in a five-hour workshop.

Kagan observed, from replaying video to guest speakers at his university (a novelty in that era), that speakers recalled unspoken thoughts, fantasies and feelings when they saw themselves replayed, and were happy to express them to him as he was a bystander who treated them with the respect given to an important speaker. From this he developed the idea that if students could record and replay interviews, teaching sessions and group sessions, and could replay them with a 'respectful person' who was not involved in teaching or assessing them, they would be able to recall some of their inner unspoken awareness both of what was happening inside themselves and what was happening between themselves and the client or clients. So was born IPR along with the role of 'inquirer' – the respectful observer who is not concerned with the video/audio-tape being replayed but is there to help the 'recaller' deepen his or her understanding by asking appropriate questions.

The counsellor makes a video or audio-tape of a session and replays it with an inquirer. The counsellor is in charge of the tape and stops it whenever he remembers something going on in him, or between him and the client, which is unspoken. He explores this himself and the inquirer can help by asking questions which may deepen his exploration but not by probing or putting in her opinions. She is neutral and is not judging or assessing the counsellor The counsellor can also be helped to put into words what he might have said if it was appropriate.

When he began to use this process Kagan realized that many students were not in touch with their feelings, with thoughts and fantasies only half experienced, and were not able to express them. He also noticed that many interpersonal interactions aroused anxiety which took attention from the client. To develop this awareness he made some brief scenes on video of clients speaking to the camera in various states of emotion and situations. He originally used students to make the videos, but later used professional actors who produced some powerful vignettes. He used these vignettes with students who were divided into groups of three, and after each vignette asked to share in their small group what bodily feelings, thoughts, fantasies and emotions they experienced. The vignette was then played again and they were asked to share what they might say or do if they were there with the client.

The Workshop

From my early work with Kagan I developed a workshop which extends and adapts his ideas, and improvises when conditions, time and resources are not ideal.

Resources: One room to hold up to 24 students if I am working with a co-tutor and 12 spaces where pairs of students can use a tape-recorder without overhearing another pair – often difficult but all sorts of spaces can be used. Arrange beforehand for students to have at least one tape-recorder between two, making sure it will work on battery or that there are electric sockets available and the tape-recorders have the necessary adaptors, and to have one audiotape each.

- Prepare handouts (see Table A1.2 for ideas) for:
  (a) explaining the Recall process;
  (b) the role of inquirer and questions to use.
- Prepare video or audio-tapes of four or five vignettes of client statements. If video make sure a video-recorder with large screen is available.
- Prepare a brief counselling session of yourself with a client on audio or video which you can use to demonstrate the method.

Session:

1. Introduce the method and explain the structure for the day. The students will be using their own material as clients, and hearing each other's tapes, so confidentiality is important throughout the day and after.

2. Start with an awareness exercise: scanning the body (can lead this by going round the body identifying all the parts outside and in), relaxing, watching breathing, watching thoughts, watching emotions, visualizing a beautiful place to go to, using all the senses to experience it, go back to watching thoughts, breathing and back to

Table A1.2 *Interpersonal Process Recall*

Interpersonal Process Recall

A method of individualized self-learning, a self-discovery process

In any interaction we pick up many cues from the other person, most of which we are only half aware of. Feelings, thoughts and bodily reactions flash through us at great speed. Some we suppress, some puzzle us and some we communicate to the other person, but we are probably only half conscious of most of what is going on inside us. All of it is potentially useful.

Awareness of your senses, body sensations, thought patterns, images, fantasies, self-talk (your inner conversations – and the ability to explore these – is best developed by having the opportunity of monitoring your internal processing in an atmosphere free of external judgement, e.g. with a supervisor, and with increasing internal self-acceptance.

IPR was developed by Norman Kagan at Michigan State University in the early days of video. Professors who had been videoed asked to see their 'performance' and Kagan, who was only a respectful onlooker, noticed how much of their internal processes they remembered and remarked upon. From this he developed the IPR method, videoing sessions and inviting the counsellor to replay it in the presence of another person. The counsellor decided when she stopped the tape and what she recalled. Kagan developed the role of the Inquirer, a neutral person who asked questions when the counsellor was recalling to help to deepen the counsellor's awareness of the process.

Inquirer Leads

Inquirer leads to help the recaller deepen awareness of feelings, thoughts, bodily sensations, images, fantasies in interaction with a client or supervisee – choose ones that seem to be appropriate.

As you recall the specific interaction

What thoughts were going through your mind?
What emotions – any others below that?
What did you sense in your body? Where?
Anything about your breathing?
Was there anything you wanted to do?
What did you imagine the other person was thinking about you?
Was there anything you wanted them to think/feel about you?
What did you imagine the other person really wanted of you?
Were there any risks involved?
Did you have any fantasies or images about the other – or about the outcomes?
Were there any images going through your mind?

At the end of the session

Anything you did that pleased you?
Anything you did which is ordinarily difficult for you?
What enabled you to do it this time?
What kind of image were you aware of projecting? Is that the image you wanted to project?

the room. Talk to a partner about the experience. Encourage the use of this exercise during the day, and its regular use, in part or whole. I have found this exercise increases the learning from the vignette exercise.

3. Divide the group into threes, explain the vignette procedure. Watch or listen to each statement, check awareness of body etc. and share experiences in small group. Watch again and decide on a response and share that. Bring the group back together and ask for comments. (Students are usually surprised how differently different people respond to the same stimulus and there is useful learning in this.)

4. Teach the 'recall' process and the 'inquirer' role by demonstration, using the session you have made and having another trainer play the inquirer role. If no other trainer, teach Inquirer role first and ask a student to volunteer to work with you, or get a student to make the counselling session beforehand and do the recall with you as inquirer, or show a video or audio-tape of the process. Give out handouts of the recall process, the inquirer role and inquirer suggested questions. Allow time for questions and clarification.

5. Write up on flip-chart and explain the logistics of the recall process and get cooperation from the group to keep to time and return to the main room punctually between rounds.

Round 1. *A*s are counsellors
*B*s are clients for a 15/30 minute recorded counselling session
Round 2. *A*s do the recall
*B*s are inquirers but for another counsellor; 20/40 minutes
Round 3. *B*s are counsellors
*A*s are clients but in a different pair from round 1; 15/30 minutes
Round 4. *B*s do the recall
*A*s are inquirers for another counsellor; 20/40 minutes (Put in times depending the length of the workshop).

The students work in four different pairs and must return to the main room to change over.

6. Set up the pairs. I usually ask the students to stand in two circles, *A*s on the inside facing a partner, barn-dance fashion. That is the first pair. They return to this formation each time and one circle moves on so that they change partners for each round. Remind them to check tape recorders before starting, and it is their responsibility to erase tapes at the end of the day.

7. Between rounds 2 and 3 it is useful to bring the group together to see if there are any queries and to get comments on how the process is going, what is being learnt.
8. After round 4 bring the group back together; give an opportunity for students to write down some of their learning, to share it with yet another partner and to consider how they will continue this learning and how they will use it in their counselling. Then have some exchange in the big group. Summarize the learning if this is useful, or your style!
9. Ask for feedback on you and on the workshop and end.

If time and space preclude students making tapes during the workshop, they need to bring a taped session made with a client – a colleague or real client if permission is given.

An alternative exercise which needs a different structure, is for both counsellor and client to replay together, either of them stopping the tape and sharing unspoken thoughts and feelings, with an inquirer to help them both. Mearns (1994) recommends this method with a real client, without the Inquirer. If the session is recorded and replayed at the next session it can 'create an enormous amount of therapeutic material'.

Video is obviously an advantage, but unless you have access to lavish equipment and technicians to set it up, it is usually not practical. I have on occasions used a mixture of audio and video. If neither is possible, I have run short workshops where the students do a session with each other without recording and then move to an inquirer and recall without the help of a tape. This can provide some good learning and can be fitted into short training sessions.

When the students have learnt and practised the method they can set up sessions for themselves using actual client material. This is a good build up to supervision and can be an addition to supervision during the course. It can also be used as part of supervision at times, either in group or individual supervision. A student brings a tape, or part of a tape and the supervisor changes role and acts as inquirer.

The inquirer role needs careful teaching to stay neutral, not get involved in the 'case', and not using counselling skills, but by questions help the counsellor deepen their awareness. I used to train inquirers to sit with their back to the video display or to try and not listen too hard to the audio-tape, so that their focus was on the counsellor and what he or she was wanting from the recall.

I think IPR helps students develop their congruence and to recognize what emotions belong to them and what to the clients, and I find in supervision that students who have had experience of IPR are more able to recognize transference and counter-transference and use it to explore their relationship with the client, even if they do not use these concepts.

COACHING CIRCLES

This is a technique which can be adapted for a range of skills training, but I describe it used as a basic empathy exercise. It is ideal for a group of 10 or 12 but can be used with only 6.

You need a client willing to present an issue and a manager of the process. If you are lucky enough to have a co-trainer, it is useful for the trainers to take both roles; if not do both roles yourself or ask for a volunteer client. If you take both roles yourself you will have to come out of the role of client to teach and manage, but it can be done. The volunteer client needs to be assertive enough, and sensitive enough to 'feel' the level of the responses. If a role-played client is used it is important for the 'player' to be closely identified with the role in order to 'feel' the accuracy, or not, of the responses.

If the students are not clear what a basic empathy response is, demonstrate it before you start the exercise, either live or using an audio- or video-tape. Some trainers use Carkhuff's five levels of responses to help students discriminate the differences (see below). If you find it a better way of learning, let them learn by doing and feedback in the exercise. Sometimes this is too shaming if students think they ought to be able to do it.

The exercise:

1. Ask for six volunteer counsellors to sit in a circle, with six coaches sitting behind them.
2. The client presents the issue, talking for about three or four minutes. The counsellors listen and each one then in turn makes a basic empathic response to the client, if possible not repeating each other. Counsellors may pass or ask their coach for help.
3. The client responds non-verbally to each response showing whether it felt empathic or not. (My co-trainer calls the good response 'getting the noddy-jackpot'.) If they do not get it right they have another go, with the help of the coach if they choose. The manager may point out, or get the group to recognize why some responses do not get the jackpot. If Carkhuff's response levels have been learnt, this helps students identify the subtleties of 'good' and 'poor' responses.
4. The client then chooses one response and goes on talking. The client can ask for the first responses to be repeated if necessary.
5. The counsellors respond as before. If the client has been very brief they may not be able to find six different responses but they can try, and the process is repeated as above.

The exercise can go on until it is clear everybody in the group can make very accurate empathic responses. The coaches can become the counsellors at some point. The client may respond to two or more of the accurate responses in any round, showing how different responses may lead to different paths of exploration and this can be discussed in the group.

Carkhuff (1969) used a scale of 1–5 to identify levels of response on any skill. Level 3 puts back to the client on the level it is spoken; level 2 takes something away from the client's words; level 1 is right off beam, not hearing and not understanding; level 4 picks up something the client may be only inferring; level 5 picks up a deeper meaning for the client (a deeper empathic response). This scale can be used for giving feedback and for exploring the appropriateness of responses at different stages of the counselling. The exercise above requires the students to give an accurate Level 3 empathic response, a skill which can empower and leave the client to do the work. Counsellors sometimes get too good at levels 4 and 5 and forget the importance of this basic skill.

Carkhuff (1969a) gives some exercises to test students' discrimination of different levels of response. These are 30 statements with responses to each and the student has to identify the different levels. There are enough statements to use as a pre- and post-test of skill learning if you want to evaluate your teaching.

The exercise can be used to practise levels 4 and 5, and can be a progression from the one above. And it can be adapted creatively to work on more complex skills. The idea of coaching, used in a variety of skills work, can help to build confidence and reinforce the norm of students helping each other learn.

COUNSELLING CIRCLES

This is a very useful exercise early on in skills training.

Structure. Students sit in two circles, facing each other. The inside circle will be clients first; the outside counsellors.

Method. The 'clients' decide on an issue or problem which they are willing to explore. The counsellors have three minutes with each client and then move on to the next client. The clients continue with their issue and the counsellor responds to whatever the client brings.

This continues until each counsellor has counselled each client in the circle. The clients then write feedback for each counsellor: how they experienced them, whether they felt accepted, heard, attended to, understood etc., what they liked, anything they did not like. The feedback is not given to the counsellors until the end of the exercise. After a short break the circle is reformed with new clients on the inside circle and the exercise is repeated.

The feedback is given out and ten minutes given for reading and reflecting. For debriefing, the students then meet in pairs and talk about their feedback, or their feelings about the feedback and the exercise. They then come back to the whole group and there is an opportunity to share the learning and to clarify individual feedback if needed.

The exercise usually produces a lot of learning. As clients the students experience a range of counsellors and can identify quite subtle differences in the way they are 'counselled', and in the feelings this evokes in them. As counsellors they receive a range of feedback, and because it is written it is not so threatening as being given publicly; they can share it or not. The very short sessions mean that they are not so worried about getting stuck and they can be aware how differently they feel with different clients.

One of the attributes we have noticed about counsellors who do well in short-term work is the ability to set up a relationship very rapidly – to convey warmth and attention without overpowering the client. This may identify students who can do this easily and help others explore what is it they do which promotes this rapid relationship building.

APPENDIX 2

Diploma in Integrative Psychosynthesis Competencies assessment forms

These forms for the assessment of competencies were developed by The Communication and Counselling Foundation for a BAC-recognized Diploma course in Integrative Psychosynthesis Counselling.

DIPLOMA IN INTEGRATIVE PSYCHOSYNTHESIS COMPETENCIES ASSESSMENT

YEAR 1

COMPETENCIES	SELF-ASSESSMENT			CCF ASSESSMENT			PEER FEEDBACK		
	1	2	3	1	2	3	1	2	3
Ability to:									
1 Conduct an interview									
2 Establish a counselling frame with clear contract, including time, space and money boundaries									
3 Establish clear relationship where counsellor's intention is explicit and shared									
4 Communicate genuineness									
5 Communicate unconditional positive regard									
6 Make empathic responses									
7 Listen to both the words and the energy behind the words									
8 Mirror the client's experience back to them									
9 Recognize and stand back from own feelings and thoughts and be able to distinguish them from client's experience									
10 Understand basic psychosynthesis theory model									
11 Use this model to work with process of the client									
12 Understand the context of abuse and deprivation and its consequences on the client and be able to view client within this context									

KEY: 1 = no competency demonstrated; 2 = some competency demonstrated; 3 = good-enough competency demonstrated

DIPLOMA IN INTEGRATIVE PSYCHOSYNTHESIS COMPETENCIES ASSESSMENT

YEAR 2

COMPETENCIES	SELF-ASSESSMENT			CCF ASSESSMENT			PEER FEEDBACK		
	1	2	3	1	2	3	1	2	3
Ability to:									
1 Build on competencies of year 1									
2 Evaluate clients in relation to the intake guidelines									
3 Formulate and hold a hypothesis about the client									
4 Make interventions informed by hypotheses									
5 Make interpretative interventions from hypotheses									
6 Work from the context of self-realization									
7 Disidentify from the counselling process and see the whole or gestalt									
8 Develop rapport									
9 Recognize and work with transference									
10 Recognize, take responsibility for and work with counter-transference									
11 Understand the effects of cultural context of the client									
12 See client's issues in larger context of their life journey as a whole									
Please add below a list of previous year's competencies graded 1 or 2									

KEY: 1 = no competency demonstrated; 2 = some competency demonstrated; 3 = good-enough competency demonstrated

DIPLOMA IN INTEGRATIVE PSYCHOSYNTHESIS COMPETENCIES ASSESSMENT

YEAR 3

COMPETENCIES	SELF-ASSESSMENT			CCF ASSESSMENT			PEER FEEDBACK		
	1	2	3	1	2	3	1	2	3
Ability to:									
1 Build on competencies of years 1 and 2									
2 Assess clients in relation to the intake guidelines									
3 Formulate and hold hypothesis from information communicated both and unconsciously									
4 Work with and evoke unconscious material through dream and imagery									
5 Work through interpretation of the transference									
6 Work with the counter-transference both authentically and interpretatively									
7 Carry out one's own research									
8 Extrapolate from one's own work with clients and research to articulate understanding and ideas									
9 Develop the 'I–thou' relationship									
10 Demonstrate the ability to build and maintain a counselling practice									
11 Integrate own model									
12 Use this model with clients									
Please add below a list of previous year's competencies graded 1 or 2									

KEY: 1 = no competency demonstrated; 2 = some competency demonstrated; 3 = good-enough competency demonstrated

© Copyright THE COMMUNICATION AND COUNSELLING FOUNDATION 1995

ASSESSMENT OF COUNSELLING AND FEEDBACK SKILLS

Given to _____   By _____

skills seen	competent	making progress	needs more practice
accurate paraphrasing			
accurate reflection of feelings			
accurate summarizing			
wide vocabulary			
uses metaphors			

Non-verbal attending (tick any that apply and add you own)

body	relaxed, too relaxed, tense, fidgets, immobile, matches
facial expression	warm, cool, impassive, matching
voice tone	
pacing	

demonstrated	very much	much	some	not sure
empathy				
acceptance				
genuineness				

Any comments

_____

_____

_____

_____

_____

_____

Skills of Giving Feedback

Comments on this group member's skill at giving feedback – this might include:

specific, remembers actual words/phrases/actions, gives feedback constructively, clearly, directly, diffidently, obscured, with care, too general, could be more direct, avoids giving negative, observes non-verbal, body language, tone, pace.

References

Baker, S. and Daniels, T. (1989). 'Integrating research on the microcounseling program: a meta analysis', *Journal of Counseling and Clinical Psychology*, 45, 257–66.

Baker, S.B., Daniels, T.G. and Greeley, A.T. (1990). 'Systematic Training of Graduate-Level Counsellors: Narrative and Meta-Analytic Reviews of Three Major Programs', *The Counseling Psychologist*, Vol.18, No.3, July 1990, 355–421.

Bandura, A. (1969). *Principles of Behavior Modification.* New York: Holt Rinehart and Winston.

Belenky, M. *et al.* (1986). *Women's Ways of Knowing.* New York: Basic Books.

Bion, W.R. (1961). *Experiences in Groups.* Tavistock Publications.

Bond, T. (1993). *Standards and Ethics for Counselling in Action.* London: Sage.

British Association for Counselling (1995). *AVA Catalogue.* Rugby: BAC.

British Association for Counselling (1990). *The Recognition of Counsellor Training Courses.* Rugby: BAC.

British Association for Counselling (1994). *Code of Ethics and Practice for Trainers in Counselling and Counselling Skills.* Rugby: BAC.

British Association for Counselling (1992). *Code of Ethics and Practice for Counsellors.* Rugby: BAC.

Carkhuff, R.R. (1969a). *Helping and Human Relations 1: Selection and Training.* New York: Holt Rinehart and Winston.

Carkhuff, R.R. (1969b). *Helping and Human Relations 2: Practice and Research.* New York: Holt Rinehart and Winston.

Carkhuff, R. and Berenson, B.G. (1976). *Teaching as Treatment.* Amherst: Human Resource Development Press.

Clarkson, P. (1994). *The Achilles Syndrome, Overcoming the Secret Fear of Failure.* Shaftesbury: Element.

Connor, M. (1994). *Training the Counsellor, An Integrative Model*. London and New York: Routledge.

Culley, S. (1991). *Integrative Counselling Skills in Action*. London: Sage.

Dainow, S. and Bailey, C. (1988). *Developing Skills with People*. Chichester: Wiley and Sons.

Dryden, W. and Feltham, C. (1992). *Brief Counselling*. Buckingham: Open University Press.

Dryden, W. and Feltham C. (1994). *Developing Counsellor Training*. London: Sage.

Dryden, W. and Thorne, B. (eds), (1991). *Training and Supervision for Counselling in Action*. London: Sage.

Egan, G. (1975). *The Skilled Helper: A Model for Systematic Helping and Interpersonal Relating*. Pacific Grove, California: Brooks/Cole Publishing Co.

Egan, G. (1994). *The Skilled Helper*. Pacific Grove, California: Brooks/Cole Publishing Co.

Egan, G. (1994). *Exercises in Helping Skills – A Training Manual*. Pacific Grove, California: Brooks/Cole Publishing Co.

Egan, G. and Cowan, M. (1979). *People in Systems*. Pacific Grove, California: Brooks/Cole Publishing Co.

Gilmore, S. (1973). *The Counsellor in Training*. Englewood Cliffs, New Jersey: Prentice-Hall.

Henderson, P. (1989). *Promoting Active Learning*. Cambridge: National Extension College.

Honey, P. (1986). *The Manual of Learning Styles*. P. Honey, Maidenhead.

Inskipp, F. (1993). *Counselling: The Trainers Handbook*. Cambridge: NEC.

Inskipp, F. and Proctor, B. (1988). Skills for Supervising and Being Supervised. St. Leonards-on-Sea: Alexia Publications.

Inskipp, F. and Proctor, B. (1994). *Making the Most of Supervision*. Twickenham: Cascade.

Ivey, A E (1971). *Microcounseling: Innovations in Interviewing Training*. Springfield: Charles C. Thomas.

Kagan, N. (1975). *Influencing Human Interaction*. Washington: American Personnel and Guidance Association.

Kirschenbaum, H. (1977). *Advanced Value Clarification*. La Jolla: University Associates.

Kolb, D. (1976). *Learning Style Inventory. Self-Scoring Test and Interpretation Booklet*. Boston: McBer and Co.

Lambert, M.J. (1989). 'The individual therapist's contribution to psycho-therapy process and outcome', *Clinical Psychology Review*, **9**, 469–85.

McMahon, G. (1994). *Setting Up Your Own Private Practice*. Cambridge: NEC.

McNamee, S. and Gergen, K.J. (1992). *Therapy as Social Construction*. London: Sage.

Mearns, D. (1994). *Developing Person-centred Counselling*. London: Sage.

Passons, W.R. (1975). *Gestalt Approaches in Counseling*. New York: Holt Rinehart and Winston.

Robinson, W.L. (1974). 'Conscious competency – the mark of a competent instructor'. *Personnel Journal*, **53**, 538–9.

Rogers, C.R. (1957). 'The necessary and sufficient conditions of therapeutic change', *Journal of Counseling*, **21**, 95–103.

Rogers, C.R. (1980). *A Way of Being*. Boston: Houghton Mifflin Co.

Russell, J. and Dexter, G. (1993). 'Menage a trois: accreditation, NVQs and BAC', *Counselling*, **4**(4), 266–9.

Russell, J., Dexter, G. and Bond, T. (1992). *Differentiation Project – Summary Report*. The Advice, Guidance and Counselling Lead Body Secretariat, c/o Julie Janes Associates, Welwyn.

Speedy, J. (1993). *Heroines, Healers, Harlots, and Hags*. Unpublished MSc Thesis, University of Bristol.

Stoltenberg, C. and Delworth, U. (1987). *Supervising Counselors and Therapists: A Developmental Approach*. San Francisco: Jossey–Bass.

Strong, S. R. (1968). 'Counseling: an interpersonal influence process', *Journal of Counseling Psychology*, **15**, 215–24.

Truax, C.B. and Carkhuff, R.R. (1967). *Towards Effective Counseling and Psychotherapy: Training and Practice*. Chicago: Aldine Pub. Co.

Tuckman, B.W. (1965). 'Development sequences in small groups', *Psychological Bulletin*, **63**(6), 384–99.

Index